Spiritual Self-Care for Black Women:

Powerful Spiritual Guide & Workbook to Help you Transform Your Life in 12 Months. Find Inner Peace and Happiness and Become Badass.

Introduction

Disclaimer!

CHAPTER ONE   9
IT'S NOT A COINCIDENCE!

Journey to Self in Relation to Spirituality

  What is Spirituality?   10

    What Defines Your Happiness?   11

      What Should Define Your Happiness?   13

        What's the Essence of Spirituality?   14

          Who Is A Spiritual Person?   17

Spirituality And Emotional Health   18

  Key Points   20

CHAPTER TWO   21
KNOW YOURSELF!

Understanding Spirituality for Yourself.

Never Stop being You!   27

Mistakes   28

Learn! Don't Linger!   29

Let Go! Don't Force it!   30

Key Points ... 32

CHAPTER THREE ... 33
IT'S ALL IN YOUR HANDS
LIVING ISN'T EASY ... 38
Key Points ... 40

CHAPTER FOUR ... 41
BUILDING UP YOUR SPIRITUAL ENERGY
Be Intentional ... 42
Face your Challenges – Don't whine for Long. ... 44
Seek Knowledge ... 45
Evaluation ... 46
Still on Evaluation... ... 47
Connect with Nature ... 48
Acts of Service ... 49
Share the Process ... 49
You Always Have a Choice ... 50
Count your Blessings ... 50
Be Reliable ... 51
Be Grateful ... 51
KEY POINTS ... 53

CHAPTER FIVE 54
LIVING YOUR SPIRITUALITY

Acknowledge The Unknown 55

Forgive Yourself 56

Forgive Others 56

Perspective 58

Release your Flowers 60

Give 61

Trust Your Guts 63

Learn and Practice Patience 64

Express your Happiness! 65

KEY POINTS 66

CHAPTER SIX 68
PURGING YOURSELF OF EVIL ENERGY AND PEOPLE

"OVER-REALISTIC" PEOPLE 69

THE HYENAS 72

THE SOCIAL MEDIA FREAKS 72

BAG CHASERS 73

CONFUSED PEOPLE 74

JUDGES	75
PEOPLE WHO ALWAYS GIVE YOU THE THUMBS UP	76
DOUBT	77
REGRET	78
IMPOSTOR SYNDROME	79
Notice The Signs	80
Distinguish Between Humility And Fear	81
Release The Pressure	81
Document Your Wins	82
Let It Work For You	83
KEY POINTS	84

CHAPTER SEVEN — 85
WHAT'S THE CONNECTION?
RELATING SEXUALITY TO SPIRITUALITY

Overview of Sex	89
A Brief History of Human Sexuality	91
What is a Woman's Sexuality?	93
Sexual Development	95
Puberty in Girls	95
Control Over Women's Sexuality; Double Standards	97

Honor Killings 97

Shame 98

Wrong Teachings 99

Fear 99

IDENTITY DEVELOPMENT 101

SEXUAL IDENTITY, SEXUAL ORIENTATION, AND SEXUAL BEHAVIOR

Sexual Identity

Sexual Behavior 103

Sexual Orientation 103

Heterosexuality 103

Homosexuality 104

Bisexuality 104

Pansexuality 104

Asexuality 105

Polysexuality 105

Unlabeled Sexuality 105

Gender Identity 106

Types of Gender Identities. 107

    Cisgender 107

    Transgender 108

    Bigender 108

    Omnigender 108

Agender 108

Butch 109

    Gender Expansive 109

    Genderfluid 109

    Gender Outlaw 109

    Genderqueer 110

    Masculine of Center 110

    Polygender and Pangender 110

HOW SEXUALITY AFFECTS SPIRITUALITY

IS THERE A POSSIBILITY? 110

How Spirituality Can Influence A Woman 113

Sexuality and Spirituality; One Side of a Coin? 114

How Have You Been Having Sex? 115

The Link Between Sexuality And Spirituality .. 118

Spiritual Women and Sex 119

Using Your Sexuality to Attain Spirituality 122

Sex As a Physical Activity And Spiritual Practice 123

How To Get In Tune With Your Spirituality Through Sex 125

    Be Certain 125

    Mutual Affection 126

    You're Both Divine Manifestations of God 126

    Meditation 127

Motive 127

Expectations 128

Twelve Months Transformation Journal 120

Week One: Meeting With Your Spirituality 130

Week Two: Feeding Your Mind 130

Week Three: Trying Something New 134

Week Four: Achieving Positivity 137

Week Five: Embracing Nature 138

Week Six: Feeding Your Body 140

Week Seven: Practicing Gratitude 142

Week Eight: Voicing Out Affirmations 144

Week Nine: Finding Peace Amid Chaos 147

Week Ten: Read A Book 149

Week Eleven: Adopting The Virtue Of Forgiveness ... 151

Week Twelve: Adopting the Virtue of Prudence ... 153

Week Thirteen: Adopting The Virtue Of Temperance ... 155

Week Fourteen: Adopting The Virtue Of Justice ... 157

Week Fifteen: Adopting The Virtue Of Fortitude ... 159

Week Sixteen: Adopting The Virtues Of Goodness And Compassion ... 161

Week Seventeen: Adopting the Virtue of Practical Wisdom 163

Week Eighteen: Adopting The Virtue of Humility 165

Week Nineteen – Adopting The Virtue Of Honesty 167

Week Twenty – Adopting The Virtue Of Love 169

Week Twenty-One: Spirituality and Humanitarianism 171

Week Twenty-Two: Practicing Humanitarianism 174

Week Twenty-Three: Signs To Look For In Spiritual Persons 176

Week Twenty-Four: Spirituality and Environmentalism 178

Week Twenty-Five: Practicing Environmental Care 180

Week Twenty-Six: Spirituality and Mental Health 181

Week Twenty-Seven: Fixing Your Mental Health 183

Week Twenty-Eight: Practicing Self-Awareness 184

Week Twenty-Nine: Defining Your Happiness 185

Week Thirty: Generosity Week! 186

Week Thirty-One: Voicing Out Affirmations 2 188

Week Thirty-Two: Growing Your Business 189

Week Thirty-Three: Spirituality and Career Development — 191

Week Thirty-Four: Living Healthy Lifestyles — 192

Week Thirty-Five: Encouraging Words For Sick People — 193

Week Thirty-Six: Dealing With Negative Feelings: Jealousy — 194

Week Thirty-Seven: Dealing With Negative Feelings: Anger — 195

Week Thirty-Eight: Dealing With Negative Feelings: Guilt — 197

Week Thirty-Nine: Dealing With Negative Feelings: Fear — 198

Week Forty: Dealing With Negative Feelings: Depression — 199

Week Forty-One: Starting A Friendship — 200

Week Forty-Two: Sustaining Friendships — 201

Week Forty-Three: Getting Into A Relationship — 202

Week Forty-Four: Sustaining Your Relationship — 203

Week Forty-Five: Understanding Sex and Sexual Intercourse — 205

Week Forty-Six: Preparing For Sex — 206

Week Forty-Seven: Spicing Up Your Sex Life With Your Partner — 208

Week Forty-Eight: Voicing Out Affirmations 3 — 209

Week Forty-Nine: Embracing Your Sexuality — 210

Week Fifty: Preparing For A Vacation 212

Week Fifty-One – Week Fifty-Two: Vacation Week! 212

Introduction

Spirituality is a brave search for the truth about existence, fearlessly peering into the mysterious nature of life.

—Elizabeth Lesser

When people hear "spirituality," they think of churches, mosques, temples, and shrines. But, spirituality is way beyond that. It is beyond religion and what the fanatics tell you. Spirituality is a journey to self and the powers and forces beyond self. I embarked on a personal mission to discover what spirituality means in my quest for knowledge. There is nothing as exciting as discovering meanings and unraveling them yourself.

Go back to the quote in the beginning. This time, read it slowly and carefully. There is one thing I want you to note, and that is a mystery. Many people fail to realize that life and human existence aren't all black and white as some people may make it seem. You aren't just dreams; you did not meet that stranger who became your best friend by chance. You did not become like that by mere coincidence. At the core of it all, a connecting force binds everything together. That force compounds our understanding; that is what makes mystery. Interesting, right? You'll find out more as I go further. I do not want to rush through this book like it is my favorite meal. For you, I'll take my time to go through every concept, belief, and curiosity delicately. This book is an opening from myself to you.

Before I proceed, there is something I need you to know. It answers a popular question that I have heard people ask. 'What is the best form of spirituality?' Even though I believe significantly in my ideology of spirituality, I do not consider it the best form of spirituality. Do you know why? It is because spirituality is a thing people experience on different levels. There are no two individuals that share the spiritual in the same ways. It is a personal thing. If you say your spirituality is the best, it's illogical because you would only be trying to compare two mutually exclusive things. That's not the way it works.

Fanatics and shallow people who do not even have firm standings on their spirituality are born in such unnecessary comparisons. I love to make things easy for people, especially for gorgeous black women like you, who I understand and love with the most significant portion of my heart. But this journey into the deep and the spiritual is one that I can't make easy for you. You have to experience it to know it, honestly.

No matter the tastiness of the pudding and the sharpness of my tongue, it is impossible for me to transfer the sweetness to your tongue. It is for you to do. That is why I urge you to seek spirituality by yourself. Do not give anyone the chance of filling you with fallacies.

I write this book for and to you with all the love I know, my dear black woman. You may never really find fulfillment without understanding this salient aspect of human life for yourself. Sadly, the subject is not given enough attention as it should. Right now, we're all about the money, the fame, the spotlights, and whatever we choose to be after, and we forget ourselves in the process. Don't you think that's a little bit absurd? I mean, it's pretty funny that we want all these for ourselves, and we're thinking, *"Oh, when I get these, I'm gonna live the life I want to live, I'm going to be satisfied, fulfilled."* And you know, all the thoughts that come with daydreaming about our future often don't go as planned or as dreamt.

But then I'll tell you that if it so happens that you got all that you wanted, whether, by luck or hard work, all that self-discovery, spirituality, and all that you left behind, chasing wealth and fame will still be there where you left it. Are you going to pay for therapy? That's a good idea. But then I hope you're not so broken that nothing can fix you by then. No doubt, treatment is good, very quintessential, in fact, in your journey to harness the full benefits of being able to understand your spirituality. Still, it's too much of a risk neglecting that part of your life because you're too busy hustling for what you want. Spirituality is what you need, an absolute necessity.

There's a guy I know that tries to be rational about everything. Everyone says he's a "cool" guy, and yeah, I think most people that think like him and always want to see things the way they are, are tagged "cool." But then this guy would meet a new person, and afterward, he'd be like, "I don't think my frequency resonates with that guy's," or he'd talk about how immediately comfortable he becomes while speaking to someone else. On a good day, I'd like to ask him his rationale for such emotions and how he already feels something about someone he doesn't know. No matter how we try to look at life from a neutral point of view, there's always something that happens that points beyond what we see. The earlier we understand our link to the spiritual manner and how to strike a balance, the better!

Earlier spoken, we must learn to separate spirituality from religion. No matter how similar these two concepts may seem, they're nowhere related. And please don't get me wrong here, ladies, love God, love Jesus, love Allah, love Buddha, the list goes on. Still, you have to make sure that while you love your religions and what they stand for, you don't forget to love yourself and do whatever it takes to get in touch with your spirituality because that's where self-care is born from. When you understand your spirituality, you will realize many things you need to do and things not to do, people you should avoid and people you shouldn't, places to be and places not to. Spirituality will open your eyes to a whole new side to life, and your perception will change for the better. You will also realize that there are boundaries that you need to set to make living easy. There's a lot of energy you don't need. You probably want it, but you don't need it. It's eating you up from the inside, and you're not aware of it, or maybe you enjoy being sad and depressed? But I highly doubt that. I mean, isn't that why you're here? Black woman, what if I tell you that you can free yourselves from that toxic cycle you cry through every day? If there were a way I could start this campaign for infant black girls, I would go the extra length to do that. But I guess not, so let's allow them to learn the alphabet letters till we can set the ball rolling for the young ones.

There's so much going on right now, and in one way or the other, they find a way to affect our lives whether we like it. With everything going on, why do we have to be a burden and let too much noise in when we know we can be free? It's a sacrifice that's worth it a hundred times over. Change begins with the individual; the change we seek to see in the world starts with us all; kind of cliché, but it drives home the point. When you understand your spirituality, you become better for yourself and others. When you're put in positions of power, the effect radiates, and your subordinates see this, and they'll come asking you.

"You seem really at ease with life; what's the secret?"

And then you'd flash a self-satisfied smile and reply to them.

"I embraced my spirituality, and you should embrace yours too."

Believe me; it works like magic when you're deep in it. You're changing the world from your corner and spreading the light. No matter how ridiculous it may sound, the world will be a better place when every one of us embraces our spirituality.

Why am I so confident about this? You're probably asking, or aren't you? Why is this writer so optimistic about this formula? Can one learn how to live? Well, we can't. We live and learn, make mistakes and move on, hoping that we don't make the same mistakes.

And one of the things we must learn as we live is how to understand our spirituality. If you're familiar with

Grant Cardone's "Be Obsessed or Be Average," you'll know how he emphasized and re-emphasized the need to be obsessed. That's exactly how I will underline the need to understand your spirituality throughout this book. You'll see the word "spirituality" a lot in this book, and it's not because I don't know how to write a book. Nah, that's a far cry. It's the emphasis! I want you to see it over and over again till it sticks! It's just as important as regular exercise, healthy foods, and making money; it's the key to living life! And yeah, I'm so confident about it because It has worked for me. I wouldn't make a big deal about it if I didn't see the results. So yeah, understanding my spirituality has helped me in so many ways I can't even imagine. I will share some testimonies as we progress to let you see how this gospel can turn everything around.

It's not easy adjusting; it's not easy trying to get in touch with that spiritual side; it's not a piece of cake trying to embrace what you cannot see. But then, does anything come easy? The steps may be easy, but what exactly isn't easy is for you to begin following those steps. You may have resigned to fate and said;

"Damn it, whatever happens, happens anyway, so I'll just let life take its course." And then you stumbled upon this book, and you're like;

"This is my last shot, and if this doesn't work, then it's over."

In this introductory part of the book, I'd just let you know that you have a start! And be consistent! This book is not a spell. Even a bit requires you to move a wand. So this is me urging you to put in the work. This formula is a potent one, and it requires that you take action. Be intentional. Yes! It's not going to work itself out. It's a practical body of work, so it will be useless if you don't put it in the position. I'll be frank with you, I've put in so much work to put this together and get it across. So please make this work for my sake and yours. You're the most muscular woman I know. And I trust that you're going to kill this just like you're killing it in every other aspect of your life. You are the best mother, the best daughter, the best sister, and the best at living!

So as I draw the curtains to this introduction close, I need you to do something for me.

Place your hands on your chest and say these affirmations after me. Are you ready? Good.

"I, the most muscular woman in the world, aggressively swear to make the ride worthwhile. No pressure, slow, steady, till I get in touch with my spirituality and be even more potent than I thought.

So help me, God."

Now buckle your seat belts. I'll get this plane flying real quick!

© Copyright 2020 by CHASECHECK LTD - All rights reserved.

The content contained within this book may not be reproduced, duplicated or transmitted without direct written permission from the author or the publisher.

Under no circumstances will any blame or legal responsibility be held against the publisher, or author, for any damages, reparation, or monetary loss due to the information contained within this book. Either directly or indirectly.

Legal Notice:

This book is copyright protected. This book is only for personal use. You cannot amend, distribute, sell, use, quote or paraphrase any part, or the content within this book, without the consent of the author or publisher.

Disclaimer Notice:

Please note the information contained within this document is for educational and entertainment purposes only. All effort has been executed to present accurate, up to date, and reliable, complete information. No warranties of any kind are declared or implied. Readers acknowledge that the author is not engaging in the rendering of legal, financial, medical or professional advice. The content within this book has been derived from various sources. Please consult a licensed professional before attempting any techniques outlined in this book.By reading this document, the reader agrees that under no circumstances is the author responsible for any losses, direct or indirect, which are incurred as a result of the use of information contained within this document, including, but not limited to, — errors, omissions, or inaccuracies.

CHAPTER ONE

IT'S NOT A COINCIDENCE!

Journey to Self about Spirituality

The possession of knowledge does not kill the sense of wonder and mystery. There is always more mystery.

~Anais Nin

What's NOT a coincidence? You're probably asking, or you remember what the second paragraph of the introduction of this book says. It's nothing profound; you can check it out for yourselves.

Checked it out? Ok great. Now another question pops up. Why is it not a coincidence? It's not a coincidence that those things happen because there's something beyond what the eyes, ears, skin, nose, and tongue can see, hear, feel smell, and taste. Yup! It's beyond the five human senses.

According to Anais Nin, *"There is always more mystery."* 'Cus there is! I know that many strange things have happened in your life, and you can't just let it pass as "coincidence" or just "science?" Nah. not at all, young woman. There's gotta be something beyond what we can see which plays a massive role in the day-to-day affairs of our lives. And if we don't pay utmost attention to what it is and its demands, we will find ourselves at life's crossroads. We devote ourselves to learning about this simple concept at a loss on what to do and how to get by specific problems. It's not rocket science, and understanding it already sets you on achieving self-discovery. With self-discovery comes endless possibilities of stable physical and mental well-being.

You're probably saying, *"There's a lot to fight for. We're being discriminated against as women, and we should fight against that. What are you coming to say about some spiritual blablabla? Are we fighting ghosts?"* I'm here to tell you that the space you ought to create for your self-care, physical of course, but mostly mental, is like a shortcut to getting out of that bubble of self-pity. That's what you need to get past the demeaning remarks and all that discrimination you go through every day. You definitely won't fight them, will you? Trust me; they won't even stop if you do.

Now let's move on to the burning question. I think I've kept you waiting for quite a long time.

What is Spirituality?

The word "spirituality" has no specific definition, nor can it be defined through any rigid approach. There is no generally accepted meaning of spirituality because that same word could mean a different thing entirely when placed in another context.

I'll be repeating myself for probably the second or third time when I say that spirituality in this context is void of any form of religion or beliefs by a particular group of people. It has to do with the self. Just you in the room with no one else.

In the most straightforward words, I can find, spirituality is the search for one's inner wealth. There are so many definitions; trust me, it's not Chemistry or Math. Every author has their particular view of the subject, and with spirituality being relative, it would be out of place to say that one's definition is wrong and another right.

What Defines Your Happiness?

Many people find meaning in material stuff, millions in their bank account, and the number of followers on their Instagram page, engagements on Twitter, and many other things. If we look at such things from the world's view, they are things to be happy about. Who doesn't want a truckload of dollars in his account? But you need to ask yourself. "Should those be the only things that define my happiness?" If your answer is yes, you have to take a step back and reason what the purpose of life is.

If the number of followers you have on social media is your criteria for happiness, let me show you what your life could look like.

These followers are people you do not know personally, and no matter how you try to interact with them over social media by any means you wish, you'll never know who they are. These are not the kind of people I'd advise you to revolve your entire life around. Let me tell you why. There's a quote I came across while scrolling through TikTok some time ago, and it was from the 2002 Spiderman Movie or something like that. It read.

"But the one thing they love more than a hero is to see a hero fail, fall, die trying. They will eventually hate you despite everything you've done for them."

Those were the words of a villain in the movie, and I know we've got that cliché opinion about nothing good coming out from villains and stuff like that, but there's truth in what they say sometimes. I hope I'm not digressing, don't be carried away. Please, I've got the point to make.

We've all seen Hip Hop and Hollywood stars being "dragged" on Social Media probably because of a mistake they made or maybe not even a mistake, just some stuff that doesn't resonate well with the crowd. They receive a lot of backlashes, even death threats! Yes! That's how far people can go to prove a point forgetting that they're also humans and make mistakes.

You can imagine the emotional havoc such an occasion would wreak on the individual if they are constantly seeking validation from social media. They'd go into depression for months, and the so-called followers would not be there to comfort them.

You see! That's just how it is! It happens like that most of the time, and it's a cycle; it's not on yourself. I might have strayed a little, but it's a small price for salvation. I've made a point. It's your life, your book, and you'll not allow some uncouth fellow to write what you don't want to be written on it!

I could list things that you're not supposed to hinge your happiness on and what it'll result in when you do, but then, we're all about spirituality here, so let's keep the train moving. After reading through, you should be asking yourself now. "What defines my happiness?" Sit tight; we'll get to it.

What Should Define Your Happiness?

Are you wondering why it is all about happiness and not spirituality? Or you're just having fun moving on. If you're on either side, you're not wrong. Everything would eventually connect, and the message would become apparent.

I'll tell you why I've been all about happiness for some time.

I believe the goal of every single human on earth is to be happy.

Happiness is a common factor in the world. Everyone is running here and there, looking for cash, a lover, that degree, that job, and what have you? They're so much and can be specific too. You're looking for all those in pursuit of happiness. Well… I'd agree that most of these things are needed to live a comfortable and happy life. But what about those who have them in abundance and are still not satisfied. And you can't even ask me how I know they're not happy because you know too. We've seen bloody rich people take their own lives; if they were pleased, they wouldn't take it.
I want to let you know that if you're searching for happiness in material things, you'll never find it because you're searching in the wrong place. This is

not a call for you to be lazy and not go after these things if you choose to. (And when I say "go after these things," I mean legally. That should be a topic for some other time) it would help if you went for what you want, I support that, but when you neglect the things you need to pursue what you want to achieve your customized "happiness," you're going to get it all wrong.

Happiness is within. When you find your inner wealth, you've found true happiness, where spirituality comes to play.

In finding happiness, you have nothing to do with Social Media. This cannot be overemphasized.

You don't need any validation from your boss, friend, your lover, not even your religious leaders!

Strong black woman, happiness is found within, and understanding your spirituality is the only way you can do that.

I believe all dots have been connected. Or is something missing, dear?

What's the Essence of Spirituality?

As humans, we grow and evolve in the physical sense. As we grow in those areas, we need to tweak our minds and souls to be in sync. The maturing of the mind doesn't happen of its own accord as the body does. That's why we can have old yet foolish people.

As we mature, we figure out the need for certain things and the things we don't need. I'd use myself as an example here. I realized the need to be Independent when I started maturing and seeing things through my parents' eyes, who took responsibility for every aspect of my wellbeing.

Also, as I matured, I figured that I shouldn't be in any argument concerning how I live my life. I did it a lot as a child. When there was a disagreement between me and someone else concerning how certain things are done, I would argue, imposing my opinion on the other party. But then, as I grew, I realized that everyone is entitled to their opinion and choices, and setting mine on someone else was just over the edge.

It took a lot of time before I could finally adapt to this lifestyle because sometimes, even what I consider immoral would be expected of many people, and I'd be like, "Phew! You are one old-fashioned little boy, huh?" And then I'd lock my lips with my fingers and keep moving.

A lot of people get more frustrated as they mature. But that's not how it's supposed to be, and you beautiful black women are not supposed to be among that percentage of people.

Don't get me wrong, adulthood is a very crazy phase of your life that you have to be in forever, but that shouldn't make you crazy. We need a considerable level of self-consciousness to get through life as an adult, and how do you develop that? Spirituality!

Searching for that thing in your inside that gives you meaning is the best life hack you'll ever hear of.

How did it help me? I said earlier that I had to develop a resistance to arguing with people about how they should live their lives and trying to impose my style of living on them. I realized how toxic that was and how it adversely affected my state of being so much that instead of thinking about my life and what I could do to move forward and make it better, I started thinking about how wrong people were in living their lives. With these thoughts continuously ringing in my head, I became overly judgmental and always looked for a fault in everything people did around me. I was a wet blanket, carrying negative energy everywhere I went. And about people noticing I was there, they quickly left or avoided speaking with me. For some time, I thought that I was still right and whatever they did was wrong, and I didn't care. Not until the people I loved started avoiding me did I realize that I was supposed to draw the line and stop playing God. I was beginning to allow that toxic trait to destroy me and my relationship with the people I loved. I had to go back to the drawing board to search deep within. I asked myself many questions (we'll be looking at that later on), put myself in the shoes of the others, and realized that something was off.

I got it all fixed up, and everything changed. I began to judge less. Hence I worried less. It started from within. I felt this freedom of mind was second to none, and it gave me a new outlook on life. Even when someone else was starting the argument, I'd say, "OK. You already won before the fight started. Congratulations" I still do this, and it works perfectly for me. You need to experience the peace that comes with fixing a spiritual problem in your life. (This is not an exorcism, please.)

I've probably said too much, and you're starting to feel I haven't responded to the question in the sub-heading. I have, but I'd give you something much more straightforward, something you can take.

The essence of spirituality is to help you seek a meaningful connection with something beyond the physical, which causes positive emotions such as peace, contentment, gratitude, and acceptance. These emotions help you battle negative emotions such as pride, greed, hate, etc. Spirituality can be seen as a means to an end; there's no limit to what the black woman can achieve when embracing her spirituality.

Who Is A Spiritual Person?

You probably have a picture of Bishop draped in a white cassock with a collar at the neck, holding a giant bible in his right hand and a cross-shaped staff in his left hand. Or an Imam with full beards and a perfectly tied turban around his head, with an equally long flowing garment. But then ask yourself this question. Don't you think it rather strange to define who a spiritual person is by their physical appearance? I mean, take a look at the antithesis! The opposite of the word "spiritual" is "physical." And then someone defines who a spiritual person is by physical features? That's just absurd! One of the craziest perceptions in life that has been unfortunately normalized if you ask me.

But then, who indeed is a spiritual person? It's simple.

A spiritual person has a love for herself and others as a priority. In this context, that's all it takes to be a spiritual person. You can be clad in the purest of whites, holding the enormous bibles, and still not being spiritual. In the same vein, you can be dressed like a gangster with tattoos all over your skin and piercings and still be a spiritual person. (Please note that this is not a piece of fashion advice.)

Are we together, my lady?

Spirituality is mainly lived as a personal and internal experience. There are no rules, unlike many other religions. No one has the right to punish you for mistakes made because the whole process is internalized. Rather than punish yourself for your mistakes, you consider those mistakes fundamental for growth and progress. Yeah, you turn that vinegar into wine and keep on moving!

When a black woman embraces her spirituality, she doesn't need to mull over the past and condemn herself for her bad choices; she lives in the present and implements the lessons learned.

We will be looking at one more issue before I draw the curtains close for this chapter.

Spirituality and Emotional Health

As you go through this book, you'd notice that most of the recommendations on cultivating spirituality are similar to those recommended for improving emotional fitness and well-being. This is because spirituality and emotional health are intertwined and influence each other.

You may be asking what the relationship between Spirituality and Emotional Health is. It's simple math.

As I said earlier in this book, spirituality seeks a meaningful connection with something beyond the physical. Yes.

On the other hand, emotional health is about cultivating the right frame of mind, which can widen one's vision to recognize and connect with something beyond the physical.

The underlying relationship between spirituality and emotional health is that improved emotional health will open one's eyes to spirituality. I'll explain briefly.

When you've progressed to a certain level in improving your emotional health, you begin to see the need to connect to something greater. It sounds a little bit absurd in theory, but practically, it's not out of the norm. We could also say that spirituality is seeking advancement in the stability of our emotional health.

In the next chapter, my main focus will be on understanding yourself and understanding spirituality for yourself. What's all the knowledge when you can't use it to improve yourself? Such knowledge, I'd consider, a waste.

I know we're still together, stay with me on this one and let's help ourselves improve the quality of the lives of our black women.

Key Points

- Spirituality is not all about religion
- Nothing is a coincidence
- The search for inner wealth is the only way to genuine happiness
- Social media should never define what happiness is to you.
- Embracing your spirituality is the most significant life hack there is.
- Physical qualities do not discern spirituality.
- Finding and embracing one's spirituality is an internalized process.
- Mistakes from your past are lessons in disguise. Learn.
- Spirituality and emotional health are distinct but connected.
- Embrace your spirituality, black woman!

CHAPTER TWO

KNOW YOURSELF!

Understanding Spirituality for Yourself.

"Your pain is the breaking of the shell that encloses your understanding."

– Kahlil Gibran

Now it's great that we know what spirituality is all about, the essence, and its relationship with other aspects of our lives, such as our emotional health. But you see, spirituality can't mean the same thing to everybody, and if you don't know and understand yourself, you're probably putting all of your energy in the wrong place. It's of utmost importance that you do not use any other person's spirituality as a standard while searching for your inner wealth.

Wait a sec… is that even possible? Not in my book because spirituality is an internalized process. You can't even peep into the reality of someone else's spirituality. If you think you do, then you're looking at something else.

People only show you what they want you to see.

Spirituality starts from the inside and then starts to manifest outwardly. But then, a lot of people know how to fake smiles! Have you ever come across a fruit that looks all yellow and attractive on the outside, and when you mistake biting into it, your tongue suffers the sour taste? That's how a lot of people live their lives. Alive on the outside but slowly dying on the inside, so if you're looking at someone from afar, living the good life, smiling and you know, all the stuff people do to hide their problems, you'd think that, oh yeah, that man's got it all worked out spiritually, physically and the sort. While you may be a hundred percent right, you may also be blindly wrong! People go through a lot and go through more to hide their pain. Not the point we're driving at, just an illustration to show that you can't possibly mimic one's spirituality because it most definitely won't fit.

The only solution is knowing, finding, and understanding your spiritual version.

So what do we do to know? The first thing you need to do is look up on Google, search for your Zodiac sign, and bingo! You got it all fixed up. Easy as pie, right? If it were that simple, I'd not bother fighting my sleep to get this across. How would you explain that they'd have the same attitude and mindset because people were born on the same day? Even twins would think differently from each other! I've come across many of them, and none of them I've seen share the same attributes or way of life. That means the Zodiac signs would not be the most accurate tool to determine such aspects of human life. It's way beyond that, sister.

What if you start by asking yourself specific questions?

In the journey to self-discovery, asking questions is vital, and when I mean asking questions, I do not mean asking other people questions. I suggest asking ourselves to ascertain what sort of people we indeed are, and as long as we're not doing anything wrong to anybody, we ought to embrace who we are and work on our flaws. Not a one-day process, but it is worth it in the end.

So what are some of these questions we need to ask ourselves?

Ever asked yourself. *"Am I a good person?"*

This kind of question is what people would ask other people and expect to hear sweet stuff like, *"Yeah, you're the sweetest person I know," "You're so humble," "Such a great smiler,"* and you know, your head begins to swell for few minutes, but when you leave the area, they start talking shit about you.

Let me reiterate this, ladies. In discovering and understanding yourself, don't you ever give any duty to another person, not even your clergy or religious leaders? The process is all you and no one else. Give it to someone else, and all you will have are errors and misconceptions about yourself. Wild, isn't it?

So what do you do?

You sit down, black lady—just you, in your private space. Make sure you're comfortable and not in a funny shape. I'm not joking. I mean serious business, you hear me?

And then throw the question to yourself. *"Elena, Kate, Grace, Sophia. Are you a good person?"* If you can do that now, do it and notice how you'll feel. After asking yourself the question, you begin to flood your mind with so many events, and then you start to reflect on so many choices you've made, so many actions you've taken, and how those choices and actions affected and are affecting you in the long run. What do you feel about those choices?

Was it something you gave, or something you refused to provide, an encouraging comment you made, or a depressing one? Put yourself in the shoes of people you relate with day after day and try to find out how you'll react to certain things you've done. You're going to come out with answers at the end of the process. And the answer will mostly not be a yes or no answer, and this is what it will look like.

You'll figure out that we have casually done excellent and evil in the process of living. So the answer can't come out as a Yes or No answer. Let's not lie to ourselves; it won't, black ladies.

What will be the result is the need for improvement. Yes! Self-improvement. You'll find out that, ok Uhm... I said that I wasn't supposed to speak to the young guy at the market, and I needed to make sure I didn't say that to someone else because if it were said to me, I'd feel distraught. And then you'll probably put that down in your diary or something and hop on to the next. It's an everyday process. You can't possibly finish questioning yourself for a day. It's continuous. It goes on and on and on till we finally leave the earth.

Concerning what our topic is in this chapter, as you keep on questioning yourself and working on setting things right, a constant will appear. What do I mean? Probably before now, everybody has an opinion of you except you. Whether they're wrong or right, they do.

But then you probably don't because you haven't scrutinized yourself and tried to act along a line of refinement. So when you eventually do, for week 1, week 2, and week 3, you'll begin to see a pattern that gets better as time goes by. Then you can precisely pinpoint what kind of a person you are or aren't— good, bad, or most definitely something else peculiar to you and only.

Embracing our spirituality ought to lead to self-improvement, and this is what questioning yourself can do. When you take this as an everyday practice, you begin to connect with your spiritual side. There's good in everyone. Inner riches! Find it, act on it and live a stress-free life. At first, trying to keep up with it every day will be tasking, but I tell you that it will be worth it as each day goes by. Trust me.

What other question can you ask yourself in your journey to knowing and understanding spirituality for yourself?

You can ask yourself. *"Do things happen for a reason?"*

Well... hell yes, they do! Everything happens for a reason. You can't develop a specific sense of why something terrible happened to you, but there's a general notion of why things happen the way they do.

And that's to make you learn. There's no manual to life, woman. You live and learn, and you know as you live. So whatever stuff happens to you that got you messed up, it's for you to learn. And whatever good stuff that happened to you is for you to know as well.

When you ask yourself such a question, and you answer it yourself, you begin to have a different outlook on life.

You can pick out some events that happened due to a mistake you made that took its toll on you, and after asking yourself if it happened for a reason which it did, other questions begin to pop in. That's how it works. You begin to ask yourself again.

"What did I learn from this event?

Have I made the same mistake since?

How has it affected my life?

Am I a better person now than before?"

Do you see how it connects? Oh well! I think asking yourself questions is one underrated activity, don't you think so? Look at how I've managed to x-ray my life by just asking myself simple questions and getting the best possible answer I can get from myself. Never forget, it's only you in the room and anyone else.

Please tell me how you wouldn't understand a topic at school, let's say Uhm… Negligence in law. Then every day, you make a note to ask questions on it.

What is Negligence? What constitutes negligence, and so on? It's impossible not to understand it better than you will when you sit there.

It applies to our lives, women. Ask yourself questions and understand yourself more because that's the cheat code.

I hope you're hanging in there, my black queen?

Let's look at another question we can ask ourselves. This is going to be the last one.

This question is more like a concluding question after you've gone to great lengths to understand who you are.

Ask yourself.

"How can I live my life in the best possible way?"

I don't think there'll be much to talk about here. Be the you that you understand. You'll be out of shape sometimes. And you're going to be like...

"Damn, I don't understand what I'm doing here!"

Sometimes it's not out of the norm to feel out of place. But it's unhealthy to feel that way for too long. You're going to improve with time. And remember that you compete with yourself and no one else.

That's how to live your life in the best possible way. Come out a better version of yourself every day. Your down days will only make you come out better when it's over.

Never stop being You!

Carl Jung said, *"The privilege of a lifetime is to become who you really are."*

Those words struck me when I came across them at a particular time in my life when I wasn't exactly who I was supposed to be, and I knew it. When you're not who you are, no one else will notice more than you will. If you're reading this book right now and you're not who you are, this paragraph should strike hard because you know that you're not living the life you ought to live. And every night, you sit down and ask why you've been so empty and unfulfilled in your pursuit of happiness. Do you know what's interesting?

You could be in a mansion, on vacation at a private beach, on a private ship, or on a private plane; you can be living what people would say is your best life and still be perturbed about a missing piece that you're yet to find.

Embrace your spirituality and give yourself that privilege that Carl Jung spoke of. You've worked way too hard not to be living the life that frees your mind, soul, and body.

Mistakes

Mistakes play a massive role in helping you understand yourself more. Especially the ones that happen in your mind. One that no one has access to. I'll give an example. Maybe you have a misconception about someone because of what you saw them do or what someone told you, and then cultivate some hate against someone who probably doesn't know you. Except you're a robot, you'd feel terrible if you find out that the one you hate hasn't done anything wrong or doesn't even have anything against you and probably loves you.

Allow me to give another example. It's just like a man who marries a woman who fails to provide him with a child, and then he goes for other women making it two or three wives who now bear him children, fortunately for him. Then he begins to despise his first wife because she has been labeled "barren." He says harsh words to her and could even go physical with her. Although in this case, it wouldn't be an entirely internal mistake, and people who are close enough would notice.

Nevertheless, it doesn't change that it all starts with the mind, making it an internal mistake. If life decides to happen and such a man falls sick or loses all his money, properties, and other assets and valuables.

The only person who remains to take care of him is the first wife, whom he despises because she bore him no child. That man would undoubtedly wish the earth would open up and swallow him. Don't you think so?

And if it so happens that he recovers from the setback, he's undoubtedly going to learn a lesson, wouldn't he? Yes, he would! Such a person would ask himself various questions (remember, right?) And when he finds answers to those questions, he would've unlocked a side to himself that he had never known or had access to. And when he does, if he's genuinely remorseful for what he did, self-improvement kicks in. The man will never want to feel as horrible as he did when he figured out he made the big mistake and would try as much as possible to make sure such a thing doesn't repeat itself.

Learn! Don't Linger!

The peace that comes with knowing and understanding yourself can't even be imagined. I tell you the truth. When you know yourself, even the mistakes you make that cost you a lot become a stepping stone to learning something new about life.

You know, when people have made mistakes and have failed in life, the problem isn't about whether they've discovered the lesson to be learned or not. Also, the problem isn't about whether they've learned the study from the mistakes or not because certainly when a similar situation like that presents happens in the future. They would've been wise enough to say, *"Ok, I did it this way the last time, and it landed me in some unfortunate circumstances, so I'll do it this way instead."*

But then the issue is that you're hanging your head over for too long! I wish I could emphasize that enough. Too long, queen! And why the hell is that? You never thought you could make such a mistake? 'Course we're humans. We make mistakes.

Ridiculous ones sometimes, to be frank. It's in our nature to do so. We've seen prominent figures do so too. So why should you be hard on yourself because of a silly mistake? No offense, but that's just silly all the more. You're probably enjoying the sympathy from those who love and care and want to see you back on your feet soon as possible? Why not show them that you're worth loving, and of what use is the love of other people when you're busy hating yourself? Get back up and smile on the faces of those who love you.

Let Go! Please don't force it!

Winding up this chapter, I'd love to refer to the words of Ramana Maharshi where he said,

"Let what comes come. Let what goes go. Find out what remains."

As we progress, we acquire, and we shed. What makes us who we are is remaining when the trimming is done.

I believe that sometimes, we look back into our past lives and remember some things we had which we have no more, and then we probably fake a short smile or something. It can be a person or an interest.

Make sure you don't force any of them. Telling yourself the truth will also help a lot with that.

Life is full of surprises, my beautiful woman. We may think that something's going to stay forever and then it eventually doesn't. And we may also feel like, *"No, I don't need this."* And that's what finally stays. Learn to be flexible. Flexibility is undoubtedly one of the most challenging steps to knowing ourselves because of the issue of attachment. Of course, it hurts losing a loved one, but then you'll get used to living without that person, and life goes on. Sadly though.

What about your interests? Maybe you find out something you're interested in, could be a skill or something else. A time comes when you're no longer feeling the vibe, and you're not interested anymore. It's not because you're lazy. It just doesn't fit, and we're so lucky to have been blessed with such complex bodies that we know when we're no longer cut out for this stuff, and we'd have to severe the times and the connection and the connection we already have with such a thing.

You'll lose a lot of things eventually, but you're not going to lose everything. Focus on those things that remain. They are a part of what makes you "the you" of your dreams.

Key Points

- Spirituality cannot be the same for everybody
- People only show you what they want you to see.
- Constantly question yourself
- Everything happens for a reason
- Never give the duty of ascertaining your spirituality to someone else.
- Understand that there are going to be a lot of setbacks.
- Be yourself anyway.
- Never get used to staying on the ground
- Don't force things
- Focus on the things that remain.

CHAPTER THREE

IT'S ALL IN YOUR HANDS

"It is not in the stars to hold our destiny but in ourselves."

– William Shakespeare

As a kid, I used to look at the stars and pray to them for wealth, fame, and all other "good things of life." If you've got kids that still do that, please allow them to because being a kid is what we all wish for now as adults, and you wouldn't want to interfere with that phase of their lives because when it goes, it's gone forever.

However, you'd have to make sure you let them know at the right time that the stars hold no destiny of theirs. You've got to make them look at their hands and say to them. "Look… you see those two hands; those are what holds your destiny, not the stars." Although they might get a hint before you tell them, they probably won't believe that they've got so much to do, I mean... *"why do I have to do so much when I've got my mama?"* Haha! Funny, isn't it. Funny, hard truth.

Your kids aren't the main focus, though; I just thought I should chip in some parental advice and lighten the mood. After reading this, you owe your kids a duty to let them know this at the right time. If this is not the right time for them, then take a chill pill and focus on yourself. At least for now.

So, where did we stop?

Your destiny, your future. You hold it in your hands, and this knowledge makes you realize that you've got no one but yourself and that your well-being should come first. Not disputing that you should also care for those you love because loving yourself is the first step to loving others. You can't give what you don't have, can you?

For some people, the realization creeps up on them, little by little, day by day, slowly until it's full-blown, and you can't run away from it anymore. But for some other people like me, it came banging on my door, didn't even wait for me to open it before it broke the door, came straight to me, and hijacked me. I almost had a heart attack when it suddenly dawned on me that I would be the one responsible for my well-being in the long run.

I can still remember how it happened. I was in high school, looking for some money for a project, and then I went to my father to ask him for the money.

I went to him and was like,

"Uhm... Dad, I need some money for a school project." Then he replied

"How much will it cost me?"

"Just ten bucks, Dad." Then he raised his head to look at me.

"Just ten bucks, huh? Alright. So what's going to happen if I don't give you ten bucks for your project?"

I was confused. What's this man talking about? Did I need to go through all these for just ten bucks? It was unlike my Dad. Then I replied, trying to be sarcastic because I thought he was only joking

"Well... if you don't give me the ten bucks, I can't finish the school project, and then I'll fail the course." My father flashed a half-smile at me and got up from where he sat and asked me.

"And how much will that cost me?"

The room went silent, and the only sound I could hear was my father's feet walking out of the room while I stood there thinking about how much my father hated me. Haha

Later that night, he called me to the same room and had me sit down to listen to him.

He told me that he had a responsibility to take care of

me and whether I was going to fail or not mattered less to him because, over the years, he had narrowed his purpose to taking care of his family, and nothing would change that.

My father wasn't the one to wait for his kids to grow before him "reaped the fruits of his labor," all he cared about was carrying out his responsibilities till he died.

He said to me

"Look here, child; If you fall, I'm not the one who gets a scar. It's you who does."

After that, he handed the ten bucks to me and went to bed.

It was like I was struck by lightning. I couldn't sleep that night. I stayed awake all through thinking about how life would be without my father to give me ten bucks for a school project, and since that night, I was all in for anything that would improve my life in all aspects. I realized that nobody would be responsible for my success or failure, but for me, so I had to make it work for myself.

I want every black woman also to realize this. Her destiny is in her hands, so she should work towards her progress, no matter how small, reminding her of the need to connect with her spiritual self. Being a success is not just by wealth and fame. A father who has it all should be more worried about his child than a father who doesn't. Why am I saying this? Most rich people care about ensuring that their families eat well, are well clothed, and have the "best things in life."

(You should know why I put things like this in a quote.) But then they neglect the things that matter the most. What about the spiritual and mental well-being of the child?

They know that one day, the child will be independent, and even if you give a child the whole world without letting her know that she needs to be connected and acquainted with her spiritual self, it will yield more when you donate to charity instead. A spiritually unsound person will be an unsafe person in the physical realm, and then money might not be able to help such a person.

Instead, it'll destroy them more. Or don't you know that putting the right thing in the wrong hands makes the right thing bad and causes more harm than good? I guess you do now.

So when you know that you owe a duty to yourself and your child or children to make sure they have the things that matter, let the drive to learn more about your inner wealth increase. After reading this book, pick up another one, reflect, practice, manifest, and you will see progress. And when you see improvement, don't stop there and let it get into your head. Make more progress. It's only unfair to yourself when you're working hard to get something done and stop when you get to the middle. Why did you stop? How does stopping benefit you?

I watched Steve Harvey on TikTok the other day, and

he was saying, *"If you're going through hell, keep going because why would you want to stop in hell?"*

Or why would you want to turn back, only to go through the same hell again later on because no matter how hard you try, you can only run away from your problems when you're no longer breathing. If you can remember, I wrote in the previous chapter that one should ask him or herself whether things happen for a reason. You must know that you're passing through hell for a reason, and the only way you can understand why is to walk through till the end. Humans want answers to many questions, and they forget that most answers lie in what they're running away from. Some questions can't be answered by anyone else except you.

Take that problem you're going through as a question and work the solution from start to finish. And see how fulfilled you'll be when you finally arrive at the answer. It's so much fun when we live our lives like that. Don't you want to have stories to tell? Imagine how satisfied you'll be when you tell your children how you pulled through that challenging situation you thought you would die in. You'll become a superhero spreading hope

People may have answers to many questions you have to ask, but for some, only you know their answers, and you have to answer them to move forward in life.

LIVING ISN'T EASY

I want to use this medium to thank all black ladies worldwide. Wherever you are right now, know that you're highly appreciated by some random guy who badly wants to see you overcome depression and embrace who you are and some guy who wants to see you win.

Maybe I've been kind of hard on you in some parts of this book, though I try my best not to; this is to tell you that I understand the pain you're going through. We're in a world where women are hated for being robust, bold, and beautiful. All of which tell the story of a black woman.

Even a thirteen-year-old knows that life isn't easy. So this is not me about to tell you what you don't already know. I'm more ignorant than I think you are if I think I am. But this is me trying to tell you to embrace what you know would make life more bearable for you.

Now you can't physically fight those trying to make your life miserable. They're going to lock you up and make your life even more tragic, but then you have a defense—a very competent and reliable one.

Shut your eyes and ears to the toxic crowd; otherwise, you'll be distracted. Remind yourself that you're your only hope, and if you can't do something to help yourself, nothing anyone else does to help will suffice. The anxiety is just an illusion. Walk past it like a mirage by constantly looking at the brighter side. You're permitted to sulk, but not for long. There's no time to do that; you've got lives to touch and souls to heal. You can't mend others when you're broken; you'll only break them the more. Heal yourself and then be healing to others. Isn't that a part of what spirituality is about? Spreading love and light? It most definitely is.

So you've got to know yourself, woman. This chapter is like an extension of the previous one because when you realize that your destiny is in your hands, you'll have to make sure you tick the essential boxes to get you through life. One of which is knowing yourself and understanding spirituality for yourself, and not letting anybody fill you with fallacies. When you do that, you improve yourself and everyone around you, and you're fulfilled, just like I am for writing this book.

Never forget, in this race, it is you before anyone else. Knowing that women would most likely put someone else before themselves, this cannot, therefore, be overemphasized.

Key Points

- It's all in your hands.
- You can't give out what you don't have.
- Take every step to progress, no matter how small.
- Wealth and fame are not all there is to success and fulfillment.
- Putting the right thing in the wrong hands makes the right thing bad and causes more harm than good.
- It doesn't make any sense to stop while walking through hell.
- If you can't do something to help yourself, nothing anyone else does to help will suffice.
- You're permitted to sulk, but not for long.
- Walk past anxiety by looking at the brighter side.
- You can't mend others when you're broken.
- Spread love and light!

CHAPTER FOUR

BUILDING UP YOUR SPIRITUAL ENERGY

"Believe in your infinite potential. Your only limitations are those you set upon yourself."

– Roy T. Bennett

Ever tried working out? Some of you should have. I wish I could make a graphical representation of how stuff like that usually goes. I can't, but one thing is sure, and you must know that it's not a one-way journey.

You start the first day feeling pumped, excited, and ready to get that body in shape. What is it you don't do? Push-ups, pull-ups, lifting weights, what else? You do everything on the first day, and if you're lucky enough, the vibe follows you on to the next day and the next. You probably keep it up for a week, and as the following week approaches, you feel the vibe beginning to dwindle. Why? You're in severe pain, tired of the diet, or busy and have other things to pursue, or laziness has hit you already. Then you stop.

Stop? I think that's where we're going to have minor fracas here.

That's how it is; that's how it always goes. These stages must come, and then it's left for you to succumb to the pressure or be very intentional about what you want to achieve. The fact that you succumb doesn't make you less of a human, no-no-no. That's how humans are built. We got some, lost some, and then learned all we could. We want but can't have it all. Completely fine.

But then, you want to do this stuff! You want to see results! You're intentionally getting your body in shape to accentuate the magical black beauty and aesthetics already built in a black woman like you.

So despite the pain and the inconvenience, you still got that picture of the lady you want to see yourself become physically, and you don't stop. You never stop. Even when you've gotten to the point you thought you needed to, if you stop right there, you'll only be drawn back to where you started from.

I don't think it'll be out of place to relate physical workouts with building spiritual strength. Even while they're total opposites, they have similarities. You start a physical workout routine to improve your physical health while working on your spirituality guarantees an improvement in your mental health. Another similarity is that you never stop. I've said this earlier; it keeps going on and on because you start to depreciate when you stop.

As we course through this chapter, I'm going to be making a lot of references to physical workout routines since it's something almost everyone can relate to. It'll make the ride more fun and fulfilling.

Be Intentional

Two powerful words up there. You know, one doesn't need a lot of sophisticated grammar to prove a point. Any comment is powerful and holds a powerful message.

Intentionality is one virtue that everyone needs when they embark on a significant journey to self-improvement. That's one of the things that keep you on track. The picture of that desired goal you have in your head, that you look at when you wake up every morning and before you go to bed at night.

You're not doing what you do because other people do it. But because you've found out that it's something that you need to do. Before you can be intentional about something, you must have found a need for it. If not, you're just wasting your time because when it becomes hard to catch up, since you didn't find any need in it, you become lost, and you don't see any need to continue. Boom! Time and probably money wasted and nothing achieved. That's a bad investment in my books. Why not start something you can finish?

In this case, this is something we all need as humans. I spent a lot of time discussing the need to embrace our spirituality which I hope now has a firm ground in your hearts. What's next after the first step at embracing your spirituality? Don't you think there's room for growth and improvement? Of course! Nudge yourself when you're in one spot because you're not supposed to be there for long.

Being intentional will help you when you find out that you've been in one spot for quite a while. Why? You begin to realize that you're now accepting life as it comes, and you're not leading your life. Now let me tell you something. Nobody ever achieved what they wanted to achieve by accident, so you've got to be intentional while you're after building that spiritual energy.

Now I can't possibly tell you how to be intentional. You're not intentional because you're doing certain things; instead, you do certain things when you're intended. So being intentional is like a moving vehicle that drives you to go the extra mile to achieve what you want to.

Face your Challenges – Don't Whine for Long.

What doesn't kill you makes you stronger. I bet everyone is familiar with the above statement already as part of the lyrics of a song I know, and it's true. We will complain so much about how unfair life is in our life's journey. We're going to be tested many times, and when we get out of the booby-traps, we're not going to be the same person we were when we first got in there.

In the same vein, in our journey to spiritual enlightenment and fulfillment, we will face many obstacles. We will lose friends, friends who can't accept that you're gradually changing as you embrace your spirituality. You're going to have to stop doing a lot of things that would be a hindrance to your growth. A lot of things will happen that will make you question if you should even be on that path. But trust me. It only gets better. Now note that I didn't say it only gets more accessible, but better. I say this because your challenges become more challenging, and you become better. I don't know if I can call it an inverse relationship; just letting you know that you deserve all the credit for the challenges you pass through. They don't usually become more manageable; you only get better.

Now, it's ok to be scared. Am I scared of what? Afraid of the fact that challenges are going to get more complicated. When I look back at the challenges I've faced and how I overcame them, I get scared because I know that something way worse will come after, and I begin to wonder if I'm ever going to make it alive. The funny part is when I go through those challenges; It doesn't even occur to me that I thought I'd never go through them.

So yeah. Expect challenges, failures, setbacks, and trauma. But whine for a long time because there's no time. Focus your energy on getting out of it and see how strong you become.

Seek Knowledge

All the time. Never think that you can stop learning because you can't. If you try not to learn, then you know the hard way. Well, learning is learning afterward, so there you have it.

Learn from experiences. Both the ones that are yours and those that aren't, read books on spirituality like this one. Listen to people who have something to offer on the subject and watch spirituality shows. You can't get all the knowledge in one place, not that you're going to get them all at first, but at least you died trying.

Having a lot of things to do can get one messed up sometimes. So, to cushion the effect of having so much to do with little time, make a table placing priorities first and be disciplined. If you feel that you have to be on TikTok every day, make time for it and make sure what you're taking in doesn't hinder your growth as a spiritual person. A day can't contain all that you need to do? Spread it throughout your week and repeat the things on top of the list every day. The less important ones? Maybe two to three times a week. Work on your discipline with that. You're strong when you're disciplined, and you'll achieve a lot.

Evaluation

It does more good than harm to stop and reflect. You might not notice many things when you're out there making things happen. So once in a while, get in your room, lock the door, sit and meditate. Reflect. What has changed? How have I been feeling these days? How do people around me react to the change I've undergone? The answers you get are also motivating factors to keep you going. If you feel better than you were before, you will want to make it stay that way all your life.

People might have walked out of your life during the phase, but you might not be aware of it unless you reflect. Then you'll realize that.

"Oh! I don't think Matilda talks to me as she does anymore. Hmm, sad." And then you go on to see the ones that have stayed regardless, and you'll be like.

"Alright! These got my back."

Then you'll know how to treat them accordingly. It would be best if you weren't giving so much energy to those who have become uncomfortable with your change process because such people would try to talk you out of it. So please give them the space they deserve and embrace those who have found you still worthy of being in their life regardless.

How does this help build your strength? I'll tell you.

When you work with the knowledge you have gotten from self-evaluation, it builds up your spiritual strength.

I'm going to show this with an example.

When you distance yourself from the people who don't want to accept your change and embrace those who do? You'll be surrounded mainly by the people who care. And what's a better option than being surrounded by the energy you need to forge ahead in life? I'll be dwelling on this later in this book when I talk about purging yourself of evil power and people. I just wanted to emphasize the need to reflect and evaluate your growth.

Still on Evaluation...

Evaluate your thoughts about the people around you. How do you see the people around you? What do you think about them? Are you judging them? What do you feel when something good or bad happens to them? Are you bitter when they're happy? Are you glad when they're going through hell? Make sure you're not lying to yourself when you ask yourself these questions. That's also one thing that can help build up your spiritual strength. Be completely honest with yourself. It's not a hard thing to do. We actually can't even lie to ourselves. Most people shy away from the truth they've already told themselves when they know the absolute truth. So this is me urging you to be a different black woman. Tell yourself the truth because you're the only one who can.

When you've answered the questions about how you feel about people around you, ask yourself again how they would think if they could read your mind. How would you feel if you knew that a close friend had been judgmental? You'd certainly feel bad. So you know what to do. Work on that! Many people go through a lot, and if they know that someone out there like you are rooting solidly for them, it would make them a lot better and give them reasons not to give up.

Connect with Nature

I don't think I've said anything about the relationship between spirituality and nature. When you often connect yourself with nature and Earth, you become aligned with the natural living energy. You can achieve this by spending some time outside closed doors, like eating out or even taking a stroll to see the sunrise or sunset.

The feeling you get is unexplainable, by the way, but it's worth a try. Enjoy the mild sunshine at dusk, feel the energy in the wind blow through you and appreciate nature. Some form of fulfillment comes from there. Trust me.

Acts of Service

Don't you feel good when you engage in acts of service towards your community and those around you? Let's not even take it too far. How do you feel when your friends or a relative come over to your house, and you make them feel comfortable, make them lunch or dinner, and so on? If you're not expecting anything in return, that feeling of satisfaction is priceless! One might feel burdened because they're expecting some payback. That's wrong. If you're expecting something in return for an act of service, you'll only get angry when you don't get it, which will defy the whole purpose of the action.

Keep serving. Mother Earth knows how to bless you for those acts of service.

Share the Process

Find someone who will need what you have to offer and share your journey with them. It could be your son, daughter, even a kid in the class you teach, your neighbor's child, or even grown-ups like you! Spend time telling them what you have achieved due to the bold step of embracing your spirituality. You will be shocked at many things you will learn from opening up.

On the other hand, hook up with people you know who have achieved what you're seeking to achieve. There's a lot of knowledge packed in there too. Never let anyone tell you otherwise. Knowledge is still power and will always be.

You Always Have a Choice

Don't you ever think that you do not have a choice? You always have an option to do what suits you. Exercise that power of choice every day! Don't let it control your choice no matter what happens to you. You can choose joy over sadness and depression. Whatever that guy had done to you, always remember that you've got a choice to choose forgiveness over revenge. You can choose love over hate.

It's your choice not in certain situations, but always exercise your power of choice in all conditions.

Exercising the power of choice gives one an edge over their emotions and saves them from a lot of trouble caused by making decisions in the heat of a moment.

Count your Blessings

Don't be so overwhelmed by life's problems that you forget to identify the blessings it has brought your way. It'll be unfair to focus more on the bad than the good. If you're going to dwell on things that caused you so much pain and agony, why not on things that brought a smile to even it out? You'll only be damaged at the end of the day if you count your setbacks.

Victor M. Parachin, in an article he wrote, **"21 Ways to Build a Stronger Spiritual Life,"** suggested a "count-your-blessing" exercise to try for a week.

According to him;

At the end of the first day, identify a blessing that came to you from a family member. At the end of the second day, a blessing from a neighbor. On the third day, from a friend. On the fourth day, from a work colleague. On the fifth day, from a stranger. Sixth day, from a child. On the seventh day, a blessing came from an "enemy."

Check that out and notice the changes within a month.

Be Reliable

It would help if you were someone you could count on. Have you made a to-do list for tomorrow? Make sure you attempt to do up to Fifty percent of what you planned, if not a hundred. Remember I told you that it starts from within. People can rely on you as time passes if you can rely on yourself!

It's all for self-improvement, and it starts to manifest in due time.

Be Grateful

Never forget to be grateful for growth. Look back on those things that have happened in your life, the good, the bad, and the ugly. And be thankful for how they've helped shape you to become who you presently are. You may not be where you want to be. Do we even get to where we want to be in life? That could be relative, but I don't think so. So you've got to be grateful you're not where you used to be. That's like a form of encouragement that one day, you're still going to look back on today and be like;

"Phew! I made it past there then, and now I'm here, hoping to make it past somewhere else in the future."

That defines growth, woman! And don't you ever forget to be grateful for it.

To conclude this chapter, I'm going to remind you that you're only human, and you should not be discouraged by your inability to carry out most of all the stuff I've talked about here.

Show up every day, and you'll see that it indeed gets better with time.

Keep your eyes on the goal and when you're struggling to meet it, remember that if not for anything at all, you have or you're going to have kids that will need the knowledge and experience you've garnered by deciding to venture into taking your spirituality seriously.

They don't have to suffer what you suffered and what's more fulfilling than knowing that you've got them covered even as a mother?

You're superhuman, knowing that you've got something to offer more than the average!

KEY POINTS

- The journey always starts easy and gets challenging as you progress.

- Nobody ever achieved what they wanted to accomplish by accident. They did so because they were intentional.

- Always remember, what doesn't kill you makes you stronger. It doesn't get easier; you become stronger.

- Expect challenges, failures, setbacks, and trauma. Prepare to move on as soon as possible as well.

- Don't ever think you can stop learning. It never ends.

- Always look back, see how far you've come, and note the changes. In essence, evaluate yourself.

- Any opportunity you get to serve humanity, don't take it for granted. Serve

- Share your experiences with people who need to learn from you and people you can learn from.

- Never forget you wield the power of your choice.

- Always be grateful for progress.

CHAPTER FIVE

LIVING YOUR SPIRITUALITY

"Happiness cannot be traveled to, owned, earned, worn, or consumed. Happiness is the spiritual experience of living every minute with love, grace, and gratitude."

– Denis Waitley

Living your spirituality is associated with what was discussed in the previous chapter, building one's spiritual strength. These two things go hand in hand. Every concern under spirituality is closely linked together, whether inversely or directly. While trying to live our spirituality, we're also building up our spiritual strength, so this relationship is direct.

Now, what do we mean by living our spirituality?

I want to refer you back to when we said that the essence of spirituality is to help you seek a meaningful connection with something beyond the physical, which causes positive emotions such as peace, contentment, gratitude, and acceptance. These emotions help you battle negative emotions such as pride, greed, hate, etc.

Now, look at where I'm headed. As much as embracing your spirituality is more of an internal activity than an external one, what's going to be the proof that you've improved yourself? You can't tell people you've embraced your spirituality when your actions contradict what you preach. No one's going to take you seriously. You've not even taken yourself seriously in the first place because you've not incorporated what you have learned into your everyday life. That's quite unfortunate if you ask me.

So how then do you live your spirituality? Hang on, and I'll walk you through some ways you can live your spirituality to the fullest.

Acknowledge the Unknown

One truth remains. There's a lot more to life than we see every day. And no matter how "realistic" we try to be every day, there's something that happens to us that we cannot explain. That we don't see it does not mean it does not exist. Even if we don't see it, we've got to acknowledge that it's there and responsible for many things that happen to us. We would never know what it is, that's why it's called the unknown, but when we live our lives having in mind that something beyond our understanding exists, there'll be no need to get worked up so much about life. That's one benefit of embracing your spirituality. Your worry reduces, and peace takes over.

Forgive Yourself

In the earlier chapters of this book, I told you that we shouldn't let our setbacks hold us longer than they should. What's the first step to letting go? Forgiving yourself. We're all humans, and we make mistakes.

No matter how grave the error was (except you've willingly taken a life, entirely over the edge to me.) No one has the right to take your life. You don't even have the right to bring your own life. So what do you do? Go about living with self-inflicted pain and emotional trauma? I say no! I don't see a black woman doing that, and it's not going to start with you. Remember that you're dealing with yourself here, so you're allowed to make mistakes, and you should forgive yourself completely for them so you can move forward.

Forgive Others

Since we're trying to live our spirituality now, it's not about us anymore. Like I earlier said, the outside world needs to know that you're a better person now.

Not by your words but by your actions. Do you get me? One of the ways you're going to live your spirituality is to forgive others.

Yeah... forgive them. You'll be doing more for yourself than you're doing for them.

Henri Nouwen wrote in "Bread for the Journey, a book of daily *meditations,"*

"To forgive another person from the heart is an act of liberation. We set that person free from the negative bonds that exist between us. We say, 'I no longer hold your offense against you.' But there is more. We also free ourselves from the burden of being the 'offended one.'...Forgiveness, therefore, liberates not only the other but also ourselves."

Forgiveness is another way of spiritual self-care. When you hold grudges against a person, that person gets a firm grip on your life.

You're probably going to think of that person even more than your lover or loved ones.

You'd just be going about your everyday business of the day or the hour, probably washing the clothes or something else, and you'd pause and be like;

"Stella, so you had the guts to try to steal Henry from me, huh? I swear I'll never forgive you for what you did. Never!"

You know that could even knock you off balance for the rest of your day, don't you? You'll probably start reminiscing on all that happened, the signs you saw and overlooked, the chats you read, etc. Then you'd start to cry and be gloomy for the rest of your day, not being able to achieve anything more meaningful than a head-splitting headache when you wake up the next day.

Stella has presumably forgiven herself and is living her best life. Maybe she came across a book like those, took the advice, forgave herself for the mistake, and moved on. But there you are, sulking all day for what's not worth it.

Try forgiveness today. You'll be surprised at how much better you'll feel than when you're bitter.

Perspective

Perspective, in simple words, means how we view or look at things, and it plays a vital role in all aspects of our lives. Perspective can also be seen as an approach to specific situations or problems. Two individuals can face the same problem, but how they approach it makes the most significant difference and determines if they'll come out of it wholly or damaged.

I had a friend back then in college. Collins. Back in our early years in college, he was always about studying just to make his papers, get a pass and move on to the next class until he graduated. It worked fine for him for the first two years until he struggled in his third year and had several spillover courses. He was so downcast that I was affected too. I remember speaking with him in an empty class. He did so well in his first two years, so I was forced to ask him what had happened to him.

He told me that he delayed studying till it was almost time for exams. He couldn't get everything into his head soon, and he had to pay for it.

Why did he stall? He didn't consider the knowledge essential enough for him to know. The only importance of the knowledge he acquired was for his answer script in the hall on exam day! So he was busy with the things he thought were more important till the time for his use of the knowledge came, and he couldn't get enough to help him scale through.

Now, my approach was quite different. Not too much of a bookworm, but I was big on knowing for knowing's sake, probably even for show off, and the knowledge I acquired extended beyond the exam papers. I wanted to have them because I wanted to have them, so I didn't wait till it was a week before examinations before I started studying; I created time to learn, so when it was almost time for exams, it was there. Probably with dust on it, it just required a little cleaning, and I was good to go.

Do you see we faced the same problem? But our approaches were different, and so were the results! That's the power of perspective. How one looks at a problem solves half the problem if we're to be honest.

Now that's for perspective on its own. What I'm going to talk about now is how we can use perspective as an effective tool to live our spirituality every day.

It's a simple principle. The quest for embracing our spirituality has no destination. It's a continuous path that has no place where we can stop, sigh and say;

"Oh, I finally made it!" And go for a drink or something to celebrate.

If you look at it like that and keep going hoping that one day you'll find a place where you can finally rest, you'll only get frustrated when you don't find any.

That's why perspective matters in this discussion. If you approach the subject of spirituality with a sense of an eternal journey, you already know that it gets better. I never stop, so you'll be glad instead of being frustrated and wondering when the journey will end with every step you take!

"Oh yeah! I got this part taken care of; What's next, what's next?" That's how it's going to be in your head.

Then you'll take a sip of wine because why not? You deserve it, don't you?

That's just how it works, girl. When you see this journey as eternal, you will see reasons to celebrate on the way. After all, if you wait till you arrive, you'll never celebrate because you'll never come.

How have you been seeing this journey? What has been your approach to this spirituality of a thing since you knew you needed it? Have you been seeing it as a journey with a destination or not? If you have, that's probably part of why you feel you're not going to make it work. Go back a little. Go back to the drawing board and advance slightly differently this time. Trust me; it will be one of the best decisions you'll ever make.

Release your Flowers

I mean, show your appreciation to others. What will it cost you if you show your sincere gratitude to others? Not a dollar. And how would you feel if someone fails to appreciate you for a job well done? Sad, right? Maybe angry too. So yeah, no matter who they are, total strangers or close friends and relatives? Give them their flowers, girl! It doesn't even cost you a flower to do that. Do you know that a little "thank you" will do just fine?

Do you have people working under you somewhere? Never forget to appreciate them and tell them how amazing they are, even if they're making mistakes. After correcting them, make sure you make them feel good before letting them go. If you were so mad that all you could do was yell at them, call them back and apologize for making them feel less of themselves when you're in a better frame of mind. Then go ahead to appreciate them for trying their best too. It would be best if you strived to make people smile and not be the source of their scorn. Respecting others will bring you a sense of fulfillment when you see the smile you've planted on a person's face.

Even when you're having a bad day, please don't make it an avenue to make it a bad day for other people who are also trying their best to live their best lives as well. You are never aware of what one act of unkindness can do to a person, so always try to keep it cool. It saves us a lot we're not even aware of.

So yeah! Release your flowers, woman. It doesn't hurt, nor does it harm. You'll even be in better shape than when you held it in.

Give

Just a four-letter word but even more powerful than we know it. I know plenty of us find it difficult to give other people what we've worked tirelessly for free, especially money, but there are other things to offer other than the money, you know?

What about your time? What about your talents? Even advice, knowledge, the list goes on and on. Give when you can and when you do, make sure you're giving with a genuine spirit and love.

Mother Teresa said in her book, ***A Simple Path,***

"It is not how much you do but how much love you put into the doing and sharing with others that is important."

So how are you giving today? Ask yourself. Are you sharing with a loving heart? Or you're giving grudgingly? If you give grudgingly, the receiver has nothing to lose. You're the one who's going to have to go through regrets. And regrets are not suitable for our souls; I hope you know that? So if you're going to give grudgingly, it's my advice that you don't provide. But don't just stay there to use it as an excuse not to share; learn how to give from a place of love and cultivate the act of giving. Because if you don't provide, you don't expect anyone to provide for you when you're in need. Now, this doesn't mean you should offer with the intention of getting something back from the receiver; that's quite shitty too. Just give freely, woman. It's an exercise that strengthens your spiritual muscles and gets you in good shape to fight off spiritual attacks. (Now, I don't mean principalities and powers, please.)

Alongside giving, also cultivate the act of receiving regardless of how small you think a gift is. That gift could mean the whole world to the giver, so you have to make sure you receive that gift wholeheartedly with gratitude as well.

This lets the giver know that he also has something to offer, no matter how small a gift is. The thought counts a lot of times.

Trust Your Guts

I'm not the only one who has heard that voice countless times telling us what to do in certain situations where we find ourselves in tight corners.

Every person, or should I say, a woman, has at one point or another in her life, heard the little voice saying;

"Hey, you! Go for it!" Or. "Why don't you calm down and see what happens."

Trust your guts, girl!

Maybe you don't know, but our guts are more accurate in telling us what to do in certain situations than our brains are. So instead of racking your brain and giving yourself sleepless nights, why don't you trust what your guts tell you to do? To me, it's a better option.

You must also understand that your guts do not speak to you every time. So when it does, please take it as a gift, trust it and follow it. It works damn fine. Believe me.

Learn and Practice Patience

You do not have to rush things in life. You've got to learn how to move one step at a time so you don't step too early into what you can't handle. Patience is indeed a virtue, and those who possess it to possess one of the greatest gifts one can ever ask for.

Do you need to rush into that relationship because you think he's got all you need in a man? Handsome, muscular, rich, caring, and all that? Do you even know if he loves you? You don't care because he's all you need in a man. But does he need you? You won't know all these when you're rushing.

So why don't you slow down a bit and take life one step at a time and see how things work out?

What about your everyday life? When you go to the shopping mall, you're in a situation where you've got to wait for a cashier or someone else to get something done for you? How do you behave? Do you scream at the top of your voice how "incompetent these people are?" I am not telling you not to lay a complaint when you're not satisfied with your service type. Nope. But then, how do you go about making your concern known? See? These things matter a lot in living your spirituality because this is you trying to manifest those positive virtues, patience being one of them. So, woman, what do you say?

Are you going to be patient? Or you're just going to let the essence of embracing spirituality come to nothing?

Express your Happiness!

No one gets an award for wearing a grimace and looking like a monster. If you're happy about something, why don't you show that you're happy, laugh, smile, come on! That's not cool! You might not be able to look happy when you're unfortunate, so why then would you not want to look happy when you're pleased. It's hard to believe, but people behave like that and find it amusing and troubling that people would sacrifice looking happy for... I don't even know what it is!

Pirtle, in *365 days of Happiness, says;*

"Laughing carries an energy of joy, silliness, playfulness, happiness, and fun,"

Going further, he said;

"When you laugh, you immediately shift to be and live in a 'high for life' frequency—and with that, you shift everything and everyone around you, too. If you choose to make laughing your default reaction, no matter what is happening for you, you will experience everything and everyone through your laughing filter."

Let me ask this question.

Do you think about your problems when you're laughing? I don't think I do. Do you see that laughing is very therapeutic?

Stop living in that illusion that wearing a straight face always makes one feared and respected.

First off, no one should fear you because you're not a serial killer.

Secondly, you will be respected for your behavior and not how you look.

One more thing.

"Take time to enjoy small, positive moments," says **Jamie Price,**

Little things and small moments matter a lot, some of which might even be more special than the big moments.

So as y'all black bold, beautiful women live spiritually, learn to cherish the small things and the small moments.

They hold much more than you think.

KEY POINTS

- By living our spirituality, we're building our spiritual energy as well.
- Spirituality is an internalized journey, but there's a need to show proof.
- There's always that thing that happens to us that we cannot explain.
- Let go of your mistakes and what others have done to you
- See spirituality as a journey and not a destination.
- It does you no good to hoard your compliments. Learn to appreciate other people.
- Give, and while you do, do so lovingly.

- When you're happy, show that you're happy. Laugh, smile, and be cheerful. To be genuinely happy is an opportunity you shouldn't take for granted.
- Listen to that inner voice, don't always rely on calculations.
- There's no need to rush things. It's slowly but surely.

CHAPTER SIX

PURGING YOURSELF OF EVIL ENERGY AND PEOPLE

"There are hundreds of paths up the mountain, all leading to the same place, so it doesn't matter which path you take. The only person wasting time is the one who runs around the mountain, telling everyone that his or her path is wrong."

– Hindu Proverb

We're going to be focusing our attention on the second sentence in the proverb above. It's essential to discuss the role that people around you play because in as much as the journey of spirituality is internalized, and like a personal journey, we shouldn't underestimate the power of other people in our lives don't you think so? Show me your friend, and I'll tell you who you are? Never gets old at all. So yeah, it's crucial the type of people you keep around you during this journey of spirituality. You have to consider what vibe they bring to the table and know whether to cut them off or let them stay.

What types of people do you need to have around during this delicate period of your life? And what are the kinds of people you wouldn't need to have around?

And again, what attitude do we need to put on during your journey? And what perspective do we not need to put on?

Let's take a walk through them, respectively.

"OVER-REALISTIC" PEOPLE

People like this always try to be rational in everything. Their favorite slang has to be;

"Let's be realistic here," or;

"It's just a coincidence."

For heaven's sake, not everything can be realistically explained or inquired into, for heaven's sake! And nothing is a coincidence! You've got to understand that, and anyone around you who doesn't want to understand that has to go. You don't have to make them your enemies, but they shouldn't have to hold so much importance in your life, or else it will put your spiritual journey in jeopardy.

These people love to question the existence of many abstract concepts, and as a woman who's chasing spirituality fiercely, that should be a turn-off. Of course, they will make fun of you, call you all sorts of names, call you uncool, blind, gullible, and many other forms of mockery. It shouldn't make you feel less of a person. That's one of the challenges you'll face in embarking on this journey. It means that you're on the right path!

How are these kinds of people going to make you distracted? You're an adult, and you know the difference between good and evil. Therefore, you should be responsible for your mishaps. Why blame the "influence" of other people for the cause of your misfortune?

These are questions that need to be answered before we move forward.

First off, don't you think it's better to abstain than stay amid people incompatible with your vision and beliefs? You might not be rewarded for "enduring through" the influence of other people in your life. Still, if you eventually fall prey to their schematics and they succeed in bending you over, it's not going to be a pleasant situation. Don't you think so?

So why test your perseverance with something as delicate as your spiritual journey? Any bad vibe or energy detected should be thrown off the window and with an immediate effect! A lot of things require that. Don't carry the burden on your shoulders; shake it off!

Now how are these kinds of people going to get you distracted?

These people are so dangerous that I don't even advise you to be careful with them; take to your heels and zoom off!

Why do I say they're dangerous? They're hazardous because they creep slowly up on you without your notice, and one thing you should know is that they don't give up easily. They don't even give up unless you give up on their company.

They don't give up because it's how they're built. They're neck-deep in trying to be the realistic and cool guy. They might not even be conscious of their influence. They're not going to call you to a corner and be like;

"Join us." No!

Your regular conversations and interactions with them are enough to do the job. Don't even try to argue; just let them go. Because one day, you'll try to see reasons with them and understand where they're coming from, and that's where it all starts. You're not going to be aware until you realize that you're already resonating with their takes on the subject. (I sincerely hope that's not already too late.) So wake up, woman! Especially when you're just starting your journey. That'll be too risky. Your foundation is still shaky, and it collapses with any negative impact.

So what's going to be your decision today? Are you going to sit back and listen to the women in the salon tell you that there's nothing beyond what we can see, feel, taste, smell, or hear? Or you're just going to ask them to get over your hair and get out of there immediately?

THE HYENAS

Now, who are the hyenas? They're the people who don't take anything seriously. Either deliberately or otherwise. These are the set of people that would likely call you funny names like the Virgin Mary, wife of Pope Francis; come on, name it all.

When you come to them with the subject, they want to make a joke so bad that they could sacrifice anything, I mean anything! Even as sacred as your spiritual journey, just for laughs. Pretty uncool, but you can't blame them; but one thing you can do is move out immediately! They don't deserve to be your audience for the time being. Let them go, or else they belittle something as delicate as your spirituality just for laughs.

THE SOCIAL MEDIA FREAKS

While embarking on this kind of journey, you don't want to be around people who seek validation from social media. That isn't healthy at all. Earlier in this book, I explained extensively that social media isn't your friend when working towards embracing your spirituality. So why be in the midst of people who live there and derive their values from unimportant things. That won't be smart. They're going to import those values as they live by them, and that's how their way of life will slowly influence you.

Under normal circumstances, you wouldn't even want to be with people that rely solely on social media for their values. This is because social media is full of double standards. There's no real life in social media if we're to be completely honest. So when you notice girls, you roll with always freak out for the gram; that's a red flag. Run as fast as you can and pursue your spirituality more conveniently. There are already a lot of problems to face, so why add to it by wanting to fit in? Think again, woman!

BAG CHASERS

Bag chasers? Ridiculous! How the hell did I come up with a heading like that? Haha! I can't stop laughing, man! Outrageous! Well, that's for that; let's get back to business ASAP!

So who are the bag chasers? Bag chasers are the guys that are always after the money.

I know you should be expecting a "don't-get-me-wrong" next. Because why not? It would help if you didn't get me wrong here; money is a critical factor to be considered to live a comfortable life. Poverty should never be an option. But then, when you're always all about the money, not giving attention to other essential aspects of your life like your spirit that will be a lot for you to handle. Imagine having a lot of money and still not being fulfilled.

While you'd be doing great on the outside, you'd be dying on the inside because you failed to recognize the importance of your spiritual journey.

If you surround yourself with people like that, people who don't want to try to strike a balance and always want to be out there making the cash, you'll be distracted big time. Because while you're trying to bring up the issue of spirituality, they're always going to be there to shut you out and bring in some excuse that "makes a lot of sense." Because yeah, it seemingly does make a lot of sense to make money and be able to take care of yourself and your family and not go around begging on the streets. It'll be easier to see reasons to dump your spiritual journey and chase the bag entirely with the gang. After all, is spirituality going to put food on the table? Or put a roof over the head? Or put my skin under cotton? Not! But then, money still wouldn't be able to solve the problems that come with neglecting the pursuit of your spirituality.

Do you see why you should strike a balance and be around the people willing to strike a balance?

Money is good, damn good! But it isn't everything, and you have to understand that.

CONFUSED PEOPLE

I'm sorry to say this, but I've got to say it. Avoid confused people like the plague, especially when you're just setting out early in the journey. Trust me; they'll do more harm than good. They're going to be here today and there tomorrow, and you're going to be confused like they are too. You might even question your journey and be like;

"Am I even doing this right? Or should I be doing this at all?" Those are tough questions to ask yourself when you're on a spiritual journey. Because answers will find you, and if the wrong one sees you, that's not healthy. You're going to lose your guard, and if you don't have anyone to put you back on track, you're going to fall out and start thinking that this spirituality of a thing doesn't even work! But then you're the one to blame. That's a hilarious situation to be in, and avoid problems like that; you've got to avoid mingling with confused people. They're bad vibes, I'm afraid.

JUDGES

By choosing to run this race, you're choosing to do away with certain vices, and you don't want to be around people who are experts in the field. One of those things you're going to have to do away with is being judgmental, so you wouldn't want to be around people who are judging others.

Let's not even talk about the fact that you might be the next to be placed in the dock as soon as you leave the table because it doesn't matter what they say about you. The subject of discourse here is solely based on how these people will influence you if you don't have a firm stand on the grounds of spirituality.

You can't be in the midst of people who judge and not judge yourself. That's one of the things spirituality preaches against, which will make you a hypocrite.

Hypocrites are also another set of people you should avoid at all costs. They claim to be spiritual when they're not close, so what's the use? Come out clean rather than hide in the guise of chasing spirituality when you're doing the total opposite. If any of you women finds yourself among such people, its high time you saw an exit route; otherwise, you will be like them. And trust me, you're not lying to anybody else, you're only lying to yourself, and that'll be to your detriment.

PEOPLE WHO ALWAYS GIVE YOU THE THUMBS UP

I wish I could get a fancier heading for this. But I'd console myself with the fact that I've been calm all through. So this won't be too much of a problem.

People like this are slow killers. They see you walking into a fire, and when you look back at them, they give you a thumbs up and be like;

"You're doing great, girl!"

"Go, girl."

"Yasss, queen."

They say so many things, woman, don't be careful with them, walk them out of your life!

Do you know what's funny? When you get burnt, they will be the same people to laugh at you and make a big fuss out of your mistake. That's going to sting so much, you know? So this is what you need to do.

Be with the people who tell you the plain truth, unfiltered. Do away with the people who always give you approval. You can't always be correct. So when all they do is tell you you're doing great, even when you know that you're walking into the deep blue sea, run as fast as you can away from them. They don't mean good at all. They're deliberately toxic and don't want you to be the person you strive to be. Make sure you cut them off without hesitation!

It could also mean that these people don't care for you enough to take their time to scrutinize your actions, so they tell you to go ahead, not caring about what the consequences will be. These people are not fit for your journey. Take them out immediately without any explanation. They don't even care, so good for you both.

For a while, I've been all about the different kinds of people we should avoid in this sacred journey of spirituality. But then, I won't forget to mention that there are certain attitudes I would consider lousy energy and wouldn't be of much help to your journey to embracing your spirituality. I said I would talk about them earlier, so let's get to it before I wrap up this chapter.

DOUBT

This is undoubtedly bad vibes. Don't ever doubt your journey or your ability to take the trip. That would only allow the people I mentioned above to take control and ruin your journey, and you may not even know it.

When you doubt your journey, you're calling to question its truth. And when you do that for long, you become discouraged and no more interested in the journey. Don't let that doubt take over you, girl. Beat it and make me proud. You know the interesting thing, these feelings come in subtlety and slowly eat you until you're all finished and can't do anything anymore. If you have gone a little bit far in your journey, it'll draw you back to square one, and trust me, starting all over will probably be the most challenging thing you'll ever do.

So clear that doubt now, woman. Some people have started the journey before you. Look at them. If they can do it, you certainly can do it too. So don't you ever think you can't.

REGRET

People always remind themselves of all their mistakes and choose to live in them, which is wrong! That's evil energy! Do you notice that I said, "For some reason"? You should have. Now I say that because there's no reason people regret it most of the time. Crazy.

It just comes and sweeps you off your feet, taking you back to the times when you made a mistake that cost you something and makes you sulk over it when the only thing you should do is get better and try not to make the same mistake anymore.

You might even be over it and moving on with your life and your journey, but then your mind wants to flashback and relives that terrible memory of when you messed up and had to pay for it. It slows your trip and can even create room for doubt. Because if I could make such a mistake back then, should I even be here in the first place? That's how doubt sets in. You can see how one thing leads to the other and then hinders you from making meaningful strides in the journey of your spirituality. Don't you ever give room for regrets? Like I'll always say, they're a bad vibe!

IMPOSTOR SYNDROME

You get this feeling when you think you don't have what it takes to be someone or do something. And when you get something important done, you attribute it to luck or something else but yourself. It's closely associated with doubt, but there are distinctions. While primary factors like regret fuel doubt, impostor syndrome is caused by remote factors, which can even be from childhood.

Maybe your parents pressured you to do well in school, compared you to your sibling(s), were controlling or overprotective, emphasized your natural intelligence, and sharply criticized your mistakes.

You start to feel like you can't measure up and strive too hard, only to get burned out and feel more frustrated and still not fulfilled or satisfied.

The truth is, you need to give yourself credit sometimes. Yeah! It's good for your mental health. You have to give yourself a thumbs up sometimes and be like, I did it, and I did it exceedingly well! That will make you pumped up for what the next big challenge is. But then impostor syndrome prevents you from taking credits. It tells you that you're not worth the hype; even when people around you tell you that you're doing a great job, you're still not satisfied. That's a significant hindrance to one's spiritual journey.

How do we overcome impostor syndrome?

This topic will be like a bonus one here because this topic is broad. So take this as a gift from me to you, my wonderful black beautiful woman, because you deserve it and even more.

I'm going to walk you through some steps to overcome this phenomenon, and I hope you put them to practice because they'll help a lot, trust me.

Notice the Signs

Before you tackle a problem, you've got to know that you have the problem first. You can't possibly fix what you don't know anything about, so you've got to make sure you know that, yeah… "Something's got to be wrong with me."

Here are a few signs you need to look out for.

- You find it hard to accept praise even when it's well deserved.

- Even when you were armed to the teeth and prepared well, you feel like you "got lucky."

- You're overly scared of failure. The thought alone makes you sick

- You're a hundred percent convinced that you're not enough.

- You avoid openly taking credit for your achievements because people will see it as proud and saucy.

These are a few signs you should always look out for. If you notice these signs, you might be running a risk of having imposter syndrome.

Distinguish Between Humility and Fear

You have to recognize that it is one thing to take credit for your milestones and accomplishments and another thing to be overcome with fear due to taking credit for them.

Being scared is normal, but then you have to bring a balance. It's possible to take credit without making it seem like you're proud. You know that's one of the signs. Scared of people thinking that you're obnoxious when you voice out your achievements. But I'll tell you something just like one **Seth Godin** wrote;

"Humility and worthiness have nothing to do with defending our territory. We don't have to feel like a fraud to be gracious, open or humble."

I urge you to reflect on those words.

Release the Pressure

Be kind to yourself and stop questioning your ability to get things done. It mounts a lot of pressure on us and slowly, mentally destroys us. Impostor syndrome is not like a skin disease or something that outwardly shows. It manifests itself as a voice in your head, feeding you with negative comments.

So be kind to yourself, learn, and practice positive self-talk. It helps you build the courage to do more extraordinary things.

Another thing you can do is to capture those moments when the negative thoughts filter in, then counter them by thinking positively. For example, when you find yourself feeling like, "oh, I ain't worthy of this," or "I just got lucky," counter those thoughts by taking your mind back to how you made it happen, the steps you took, the sleepless nights, anything at all that reminds you of how hard you worked for what you got. It goes a very long way to help battle impostor syndrome.

Document Your Wins

When faced with impostor syndrome, you find it hard to understand how much you did and what role you played in your achievements. Then you begin to attribute your wins to fate, luck or even the hard work of others.

So this is what you need to do that'll help as well.

Have a journal to document your accomplishments and what you did to make them happen. It'll be a very good reminder in the future when negative thoughts start filtering in.

Imagine you have a book you could quickly turn to remind yourself how much of a monster you are! You could call it your "Book of Success." You might even want to go through it every day. It will make you realize that you can do more than that, and it's a plus for you!

Let It Work For You

I will be the wrong person and a liar if I tell you that one can completely get rid of the impostor syndrome because you can't possibly do that. But what you can do is embrace it, stop it from hindering your success and use it to forge your success!

Many successful people said they've battled and are still battling the condition.

Actor Don Cheadle said this about himself;

"...All I can see is everything I'm doing wrong that is a sham and a fraud."

But then, if it didn't stop them from achieving the heights they've gotten to, then it definitely wouldn't stop a strong black woman from achieving what they wish to achieve.

With this, I've come to the end of my little lecture on impostor syndrome as a gift to my wonderful black woman. Learn to cope with this phenomenon and be strengthened to keep moving on in the journey of your spirituality.

I believe in you, ladies, and you should believe in yourself too!

KEY POINTS

• As much as the journey of spirituality is personal, other people also play a massive role for the better.

• You don't need to be too realistic in the pursuit of spirituality

• Don't hesitate to let go of people whose reasoning does not resonate with yours. Especially as someone new to the race.

• Most of the time, people's influence on each other is not a conscious effort.

• Spirituality should not be what you joke with. There are other things to laugh about.

• Money can't solve spiritual issues.

• You're not always right; avoid people who don't tell you the truth.

• Never give room for doubt in the journey of spirituality.

• In this journey, whatever mistake you made in the past stays in the past. The only use of errors is to teach lessons.

• Taking credits for your wins doesn't make you arrogant. Learn to acknowledge that you're good enough and worthy of every accomplishment you've worked hard for.

CHAPTER SEVEN

WHAT'S THE CONNECTION?

RELATING SEXUALITY TO SPIRITUALITY

"When we touch the place in our lives where sexuality and spirituality come together, we touch our wholeness and the fullness of our power and, at the same time, our connection with a power larger than ourselves."

Judith Plaskow

Before I begin this lengthy talk about sexuality and spirituality, I have a story to tell you, my dear black woman, and I hope you stay with me till the end. I don't usually share this story with people because it's not entirely about me, and even though I've been permitted to share it, I sometimes feel terrible about it due to some of my past actions. However, I would gladly tell you because I am committed to seeing you grow spiritually. So shall we?

I had a girlfriend whose name I'd like to withhold seven years ago and instead call Zee. After numerous flings and a handful of relationships I had been in, I decided I was in love. I could feel it. I was sure that I loved Zee, and it wasn't even a question of whether she loved me. She even loved me more than I did, and at times it was scary, but I took solace in the fact that it didn't matter so much. It was precisely a year before

I popped the question, and she happily said yes to me. Until then, I didn't know much about her family or anything about her. All I knew, she told me, and she told me what she wanted me to know.

Skip to a month to our wedding, and Zee changed overnight. LITERALLY. Especially in the area of intimacy. It was like she felt disgusted by every touch of mine, and I started having feelings of suspicion. My suspicions were proven accurate, but I couldn't even be angry. I was dumbfounded. Zee was bi. Yeah, she was bisexual.

My initial reaction was, "What the FUCK?"

I didn't hesitate to let her know I was utterly upset because she not only cheated on me but kept her sexuality a secret for the one year and four months we were together. Without waiting for an explanation, I left her house and cut off all communications with her.

When I think about my reaction, all I want to do is hope that the ground splits into two and eats me whole because it's downright embarrassing. Two months later, I began to ask myself why I didn't wait to hear her side of the story, why I judged her so quickly after claiming to love her, why I did this, and why I did that.

It became unbearable at some point, so I placed a call to her, and surprisingly, she was willing to talk to me. We met at our favorite café to talk about what exactly happened. I could tell she was doing fine without me, probably with her girlfriend; I would never know, whereas I looked like shit.

So Zee told me that she felt more love for me than she had felt for anyone she ever dated and that everything changed a day after I proposed. A hot lesbian chic on the block that is only interested in 'straight' girls decided to get Zee.

Zee told me something vital to sexuality, which I would be talking about extensively; thank you very much. She said it was all confusing for her, getting to know her sexuality, but with the coming of her new lover, everything seemed just right. She had struggled with knowing her proper sexual orientation since childhood and while being heterosexual felt good, being bisexual made her feel the freedom she never felt. That was all I needed to know.

I felt it was me for months – that I was the one at fault. Maybe I wasn't doing it right, maybe my sex game wasn't as good, but it was all Zee. It had all been her. While I felt relieved, I could never get over the fact that I judged and almost hated her for embracing her true sexuality.

Now, connecting sexuality and spirituality looks pretty unusual, absurd even. A lot of people look at sexuality from the physiologist's lens. They're only about the physical aspects, the pleasure, and the rest. But the truth remains – a very subtle truth, though – getting in touch with your spirituality makes life a lot easier to live because you've found what works for you.

You're going to love your life that way regardless of

what anyone says, provided that you're not propagating anything evil or spiteful or even something you wouldn't want anyone to do to you. If embracing spirituality makes one live life on more simple terms, imagine applying that spirituality you've adopted to other aspects of your life; Sexuality being one aspect of your spirituality is needed.

Okay, okay, it seems I'm already boarding the boat and leaving you at sea, so I'm going to take this slow, much slower, and more detailed than the rest of the topics I've talked about because of how delicate this topic is. This concept of sexuality isn't discussed every time, and even when it is tabled, not enough justice is usually done to it. You must adequately understand this because it's a prerequisite to accessing your full girl power, my dear black woman.

When the topic of sexuality pops up in our faces, what comes to most minds is how we understand our bodies about sex and relationships. Merriam Webster's dictionary defines sexuality as "the quality or state of being sexual: the condition of having sex; sexual activity; expression of sexual receptivity or interest especially when excessive," and the Oxfords English Dictionary backs it up by defining it as "the feelings and activities connected with a person's sexual desires."

These definitions are exciting and helpful in the slightest sense, but what if I told you there was more to sexuality than "the state of being sexual" or "the feelings and activities connected with a person's sexual desires?"

Sexuality is one of the fundamental forces behind people's thoughts, behaviors, and feelings. It encompasses how procreation occurs and talks about one's psychological and sociological beliefs about sex. Sexuality is regulated by various parts of the brain, which shape the body and mind towards seeking pleasure. As much as practicing is essential to acknowledge your sexuality fully, just the slightest thoughts and fantasies can be considered ways of experiencing and expressing your sexuality?

There's nothing to be ashamed of about sexuality, as it is a significant part of being human. The entirety of sexuality is about sex, sexual orientation, reproduction, gender identity, and pleasure, so it is not out of place that either of these keywords frequently appears when we talk about a topic as exciting and delicate as this.

Overview of Sex

Sex pushes us to do many things, making babies one of the significant reasons which used to be the primary reason people indulged in sex back in the day. Sex makes us feel perfect if you know what I mean; it gives us pleasure, and you may even say our bodies are built for sex.

There are many health benefits of sex, and I'll list a few;

- Helps for a more robust immune system.

- Allows for effective pain relief.

- Helps take away signs of depression.

- A great confidence booster.

- Strengthens your muscles, etcetera.

There are a lot of factors that can influence our sexual experience. These include age, gender, mass media, race, marital status, parents, cultures, religious and spiritual beliefs, etc.

Some significant factors such as cultural and religious beliefs can influence how a person views sex and sexuality and reacts to these concepts. These factors can either cause shame or uplift an individual, depending on how the individual reacts to them.

Sexual trauma is another factor that can influence our sexual experience. Some people who have been raped or assaulted may go through depression and feel numb or hateful towards sex.

Sex can be used interchangeably with sexuality, but it is just one part of sexuality.

A Brief History of Human Sexuality

The history of human sexuality goes way back over 200,000 years ago. It's almost as old as human history. Just as creativity, writing, and speech can be traced more than a hundred thousand years back, sex can also be outlined. Artifacts recovered from ancient cultures, when examined, have been recorded to be fertility totems. An ancient text referred to as the Kama Sutra, which dates from 400 BCE to 200 CE, is an Indian text that talks about sexuality, pleasure, and emotional fulfillment. It's like a manual for sex and a guide to sexuality that discusses the nature of love, finding love, maintaining your relationship, and everything related to love and sex. Just like the Kama Sutra, the Qur'an, Bible, and Torah also give rules and advice as well as tell stories about sex since antiquity.

The thing is, sex has been around from the time of conception, but scientists only started investigating sex around the '80s until now. In 1837, Alexander Jean Baptiste Parsnt-Duchatelet published a 1830s study on prostitutes in Paris. The prostitutes were about 3,558 and were registered. That study was the first work of modern sex research.

A method of research known as the case study method came about during the 190s, and it was said to be employed by scientists in the investigations of sex. Some of the best case studies were carried out by Sigmund Freud, an Australian Neurologist who founded psychoanalysis. He is believed to be the first scientist to set a connection between sex and healthy development in humans. He believed human beings are sexual and refuted the widespread belief that children cannot have sexual feelings. This redefinition of sexuality and the inclusion of children in it led him to formulate the term "Oedipus complex." He also argued that developing a person's personality from childhood passes through five psychosexual stages: oral, anal, phallic, latency, and genital stages. There's an expression of libido during these stages and across parts of the body.

Henry Havelock Ellis, an English physician who studied human sexuality, also published works about human sexuality. Some of his famous works are on transgender people and how they are different from homosexuals. He advocated for women's education on human sexuality and believed that if women were given a chance, they would choose better sexual partners.

I can't end this talk on the brief history of human sexuality without mentioning the father of human sexuality research, Alfred Charles Kinsey, an American biologist and the founder of the Institute for Sex Research located at Indiana University. Some of his books are Sexual Behavior in the Human Male (1948) and Sexual Behavior in the Human Female (1953). He was initially an expert on wasps before he redirected his course of study to humans.

He is widely known as the first significant figure in American sexology whose research spurred sexologists to explore human sexuality. Not only did he encourage sexologists with his work, but he argued against the popular notion that women were generally not sexual beings. So we have this science god to thank amongst many others when studying female sexuality.

What is a Woman's Sexuality?

I stated earlier that sexuality is one of the fundamental forces behind people's thoughts, behaviors, and feelings. It encompasses how procreation occurs and talks about one's psychological and sociological beliefs about sex. Sexuality is about accepting who you are and all that you've experienced. It's about exploring and taking total control of your own body. A woman who's confident in her sexuality is a strong woman who can define pleasure on her terms and not bend to the whims of others.

Sexuality is regulated by various parts of the brain, which shape the body and mind towards seeking pleasure. The entirety of sexuality is about sex, sexual orientation, reproduction, gender identity, and fun.

Now, my beautiful black woman, a woman's sexuality is about different behaviors exhibited by women. These behaviors include the sexual orientation and behavior of women. Sexuality is influenced by several factors such as psychological, cultural, religious, legal, spiritual, and a host of other factors.

Talking about the cultural factor, the arts of that particular culture shows a significant part of what society thinks about human sexuality. It includes both the covert and overt aspects of female sexuality and behavior.

A legal factor could present boundaries and limits to sexual behavior, stating what is and isn't allowed in society. Female sexuality, like sexuality in general, cuts across all regions of the world and is constantly changing.

You might be born with particular sexuality as a woman. Still, with your exposure to your environment, your religious beliefs, and others, you find that you've evolved and picked up another sexuality. As a woman, you might feel a great urge towards sex, but you may not feel anything sometimes. It's all part of being a woman.

With this, we can now delve into the topic thoroughly. I hope your attention is still with me because I'm about to answer the bugging question, what is a woman's sexuality?

It's all we've been saying about sexuality. When a woman can feel a certain way, have a sensual reaction, and be attracted to people, we're talking about her sexuality. It's also about a female choosing who she has sex with. Finding people to who you're attracted in a sexual, emotional, or physical way is a part of your sexuality. It is one thing to find out your true sexuality and another to explore and express it. Ways in which you can explore and express your sexuality can be found in things like fantasizing about a person or sex, masturbating, kissing, sexual dreams, and penetrative or oral sex.

Sexual Development

Infants do not see the opposite sex as the opposite sex. They know if this person is my friend, then they are. There's no stress over which gender they belong to. You could kiss a baby, and they would giggle and not feel any sexual tension between you two because they're simply infants, and sexual hormones in them have not yet been released.

In early childhood, usually starting from age 3, a child begins to become aware of the other gender and its gender.

Biological research suggests that androgens play a definite role in deciding which gender gets the sensitive part and specific behaviors.

During the adolescent stages, significant sexual developments occur in the human body, and it is in this stage we reach puberty. Puberty is a phase of transition during which significant effects of sexuality occur. Puberty, as we know, is the peak of sexual maturity—the period where a male or female is capable of reproduction.

Puberty in Girls

Puberty in girls begins at around ages 8 and 13 years old. It is a period where a child's body begins to mature as they grow toward adulthood. The first sign is that their breasts develop and grow more significant for girls. Other signs of puberty in girls are body hair growth, vaginal discharge, menstruation, wider hips, increase in height, etcetera.

These changes all work towards ensuring the ability to reproduce in a woman. The changes can be internal or external. Puberty starts in the brain. It begins in the parts of the brain that oversee bodily functions such as blood pressure, temperature, and heart rate. The brain also produces chemicals that travel to the bloodstream through specific organs. These sex organs are, in turn, stimulated to release sex hormones.

A female hormone called estrogen is released by a girl's ovaries when stimulated. It is this hormone that causes the changes in girls associated with puberty. The balance of progesterone and estrogen causes menstruation.

Sexual feelings usually develop when a female hits puberty or at an adolescent stage. We very well know what comes with sexual feelings; the attraction to either male or female, sexual dreams, masturbation, and the likes. It's all a normal phase required for the growth of the female.

The female brain constantly develops up till the age of 25, and there are a lot of changes that come with it. This development can affect our abilities to make decisions, but we should strive to make the right decisions that will always make us feel safe.

Control Over Women's Sexuality; Double Standards

I went to several places and countries to get first-hand information and people's opinions about sexuality regarding my research on this topic. While many were willing to talk openly about it, numerous others saw it as shameful and went as far as shuddering at the mention of this topic. You can guess that women took up a large chunk of the numbers among these numerous people.

I find that there are a lot of double standards held by society when it comes to sexuality. A glaring example is how culture encourages a man to have free sexuality while a woman is told to deny hers. A man is applauded for having multiple sexual partners, and a woman scorned, spat on, and called all sorts of names for doing the same thing a man would do concerning sexual freedom. Men are cheered on when they indulge in pre-marital sex, while girls are stigmatized and shunned for doing the same.

Many attempts have been made in the past and present to nullify women's sexuality completely. "It's a man's world" and, as such, desire that women be trodden upon. Mastering your sexuality is a key to unlocking the treasure chests inside you, my dear black woman, so strive hard, by all means, to do so.

Even in most cultural practices, FGM, which is short for Female Genital Mutilation, continues today, and it's highly appalling, the least to say. I want to take a moment to applaud everyone who is constantly fighting against this barbaric practice and hope that someday, it will be outlawed in all nations.

Besides FGM, several methods have been employed to control female sexuality, such as honor killings, shame, wrong teachings, and fear.

Honor Killings

An honor killing or shame killing is the murder of an individual who could be an outsider or part of a family by someone desperate to protect their so-called dignity and honor. Most honor killings are nurtured in a misogynistic society as they are usually targeted at women. A woman can be killed for critical reasons such as speaking out as a victim of sexual assaults, refusing to succumb to an arranged marriage, committing adultery, inappropriate dressings, or seeking a divorce – even in cases of an abusive husband.

Honor killings are prevalent in Pakistan, Bangladesh, India, and Indonesia, with these countries having the top record of honor killings.

Shame

Most women are made to go through terrible experiences in their life that leave them with feelings of shame regarding their gender. Revealing cleavage in the media is becoming a norm, and women who engage in such acts are applauded and accepted by the society that calls them sexy. However, the reverse is the case for nursing mothers shamed for publicly breastfeeding their children. It even goes as far as kicking them out of public places for such a simple act of love that society deemed inappropriate. It's tiring because this is only the tip of the iceberg regarding the numerous times' women have been shamed.

It even goes as far as society condemning women to talk about indulging in masturbation. Oh yes. A historical device known as the chastity belt was used to control female sexual behavior. It's like a piece of clothing with a lock designed for and worn by women to prevent sexual intercourse. As the name implies, they were worn to protect women's virtue and avoid any unauthorized male or masturbation by the woman who wore them. I cannot imagine the level of shame such women had to face.

Wrong Teachings

The propaganda against women's sexuality is pushed when society decides to lie to the female child and give wrong teachings instead. Girls are taught to hate sex and masturbation. They are told that they're all acts of sin and should wait until marriage, whereas a boy who hasn't masturbated is frowned upon. Society encourages boys but not girls to explore their sexuality, masturbate, take charge of what they want, and discover pleasure, but neglects that women are humans and should be given the freedom to explore their bodies.

Fear

Do you know that doctors examine the hymen of a

woman to check if she has had sex or not? Girls are told that if the hymen isn't intact, they're no longer virgins and that it's a taboo. So out of fear, girls recoil and are afraid to participate in their best sports so their hymen wouldn't break, but what if I told you that hymens do not break? Yes, my beautiful black woman! Hymens can stretch and cause a small tear, but it certainly doesn't break. This is why you need to be in charge of your sexuality and know who you are. You are a queen and shouldn't let anyone tell you otherwise. You are powerful, and no one should be allowed to talk you down!

While the list is endless, I do not wish to dwell on the negative but to attend to the negative and turn it into positivity. With so much conviction in my heart and all my research on women's sexuality, I do believe if you walk with me completely, not faltering or doubting, you'll be able to know, embrace and fully express your sexuality. Oh, and don't worry, you'll see how your sexuality can affect your spirituality. Sit tight, beautiful black woman. It's going to be a fun ride!

IDENTITY DEVELOPMENT

SEXUAL IDENTITY, SEXUAL ORIENTATION, AND SEXUAL BEHAVIOR

Sexual Identity

Sexual identity has to do with how a person thinks of themselves to whom they're sexually or romantically attracted. It can also be referred to as sexual orientation identity, a term for when people choose to identify or choose not to identify with a particular type of sexual orientation.

This term is related to sexual orientation and sexual behavior, but they can be differentiated. I'll give distinct definitions first and move ahead to talk some more about each of them.

Sexual identity is what a person thinks or conceives of his or herself sexually,

Sexual behavior refers to the sexual acts which an individual engages in, an

Sexual orientation, a part of sexual identity, is about how you feel sexually towards others. It entails your sexual attraction towards the opposite gender, the same gender, both genders, and even none at all.

So if I believe that I'm heterosexual and affirm that I am, that's my sexual identity. If I feel only attracted and wish to have sex with the opposite gender, my sexual orientation. Then if I have sex with the opposite gender, no matter the race or ethnicity, that's my sexual behavior.

You see, they're alike but different. Now we can go back to sexual identity.

Developing a stable consciousness of yourself and your role in society is an excellent sign that you're experiencing a healthy development as an adolescent. For an individual to be fully prepared for intimacy, he needs to have a strong sense of their sexuality. Ways in ways adolescents develop sexually include role-play and experiment.

Knowing one's sexuality is needed for intimacy and having sexual intercourse. Still, your sexual identity can change over time and diverge from the known sexual behavior, orientation, or biological sex.

Amongst sexual orientation and sexual behavior, sexual identity is more closely related to sexual behavior. For instance, homosexual and bisexual men and women are more prone to having sex with someone of the same sex, in contrast to a lesser percent of men and women who had attractions to people of the same sex. This is because more and more people understand who they are and what they want and going for it. Gender and sex are essential parts of a person's identity, but they do not necessarily tell us about their sexual orientation.

Sexual Behavior

Sexual behavior, human sexual practice, or human sexual activity has to do with how individuals express their sexuality. It encompasses the sexual acts people engage in concerning their sexuality. These sexual acts range from masturbation, sexual intercourse, oral sex, etcetera. Some cultures and religions frown upon sexual activities outside of marriage, while some sexual activities such as sexual assault and rape are considered illegal universally.

Sexual Orientation

As stated earlier, sexual orientation is about how you feel sexually towards other people. For further explanation, it can be defined as the ability of someone to sexually arouse the interest of another person or the sexual attractions one can feel towards another person.

Sexual orientation can be classified into the following:

Heterosexuality

Heterosexuals are commonly called 'straight' people. Heterosexuality is a type of orientation where a person feels attracted to another person or persons of the opposite sex. This type of identity group is the largest sexual identity group globally.

Homosexuality

This is a type of sexuality where a person is attracted only to the same sex. So a man can be attracted to another man, and he's called a homosexual man or gay, while a woman can be attracted to another woman, and she's tagged a homosexual woman, lesbian, or less frequent times, gay.

Bisexuality

As the name implies, this type of sexuality is a person attracted to both male and female genders. People who embrace this identity are called bisexuals. They do not necessarily need to like both genders equally. It all boils down to the fact that they can choose to have sex with any gender, despite seemingly being committed to one gender.

Pansexuality

When people are sexually attracted to others regardless of their gender identity or sex, you can say they are pansexuals. Pansexuality has to do with gender-blindness. Pansexuals focus on other reasons and not gender to be romantically or sexually attracted to others. It can be considered a type of bisexuality.

Asexuality

Asexuality is different from the rest. Asexuals lack sexual attraction to other people. Their interest in sexual activities is usually absent or, if present at all, minimal. It is important to note that asexuality is entirely different from abstention and celibacy.

Polysexuality

This is sometimes used interchangeably with bisexuality. It's not precisely different as it encompasses various types of sexuality. A person is usually sexually attracted to many people but not all genders.

Unlabeled Sexuality

This is when an individual chooses not to fall under any sexual identity. Individuals can refuse to label their sexuality because it makes them feel put in a 'box' or unsure of their sexuality. I may not like the labels that come with a specific type of sexuality and wish to feel free, so I'd choose to be unlabeled. Most people who decide to be unlabeled prefer to be sexually attracted to a person and not their gender.

Some women identify as unlabeled because of their uncertainty about the types of relationships they might later choose to have. I could refuse to label my sexuality because I want to feel free. I wouldn't want to feel compelled or forced to be attracted to someone my sexual identity says I should. Do you understand, my beautiful black woman?

Overall, we're constantly developing, so it's okay for your sexuality to change. It may change, it may not, but most importantly, I need you to understand that it's magnificent to feel the way you think, and you don't have to judge yourself for it.

Gender Identity

Gender identity is related to sexuality in a way. It's defined as the conception of yourself. So as a woman, if you choose to identify or be called a woman, then no one can call you a man. And if, as a woman, you decide to be called a man, do things that men do and act like a man to identify with the gender, you would be called a man. The same goes for men, it looks complex, but it's simple.

A person born as a female can choose to identify as a man, and when they have sexual relations with a woman, they can be called a heterosexual. Still, if a female who identifies as a male chooses to have sexual intercourse with a male, they're gay.

As children, we were taught about the cultural norms of masculinity and femininity. It was common for a girl to have long hair or long dresses, and we've come to terms with it. Some cultures even attribute the building of houses to men, while cooking was a woman's job. But the thing is, culture changes over time; hence the beliefs about gender can also change. Formally, pink was associated with femininity, while blue was for boys. About a century ago, there was a revolution, and these same cultures changed their ideas and had baby boys wearing pink clothing and girls in blue.

A typical attitude towards people who identify outside the gender they see as 'normal,' such as – a boy identifying as a boy and a girl identifying as a girl or the 'common' sexual orientation, which is heterosexuality – is that of hostility and discrimination. Members of the LGBTQ+ community are treated in the most hostile manners, and some are even imprisoned and given different sentences in countries where gay activities aren't legalized.

As a part of our spiritual growth and a journey to loving ourselves and each other, discrimination against someone based on their sexual orientation or behavior and gender identity should not be acceptable. For a better society and humanity to move forward, it is only proper to show love to everyone around us and accept everyone, no matter their choices. I don't see why you should hate or discriminate against anyone for choosing to love or have sex with someone of a different gender when they are in no way causing harm to you. My beautiful black woman, what do you think?

Types of Gender Identities.

Cisgender

Like heterosexuality, cisgender seems to be the leading gender identity. It refers to people who still identify with their birth sex. So if you were born as a female at birth and choose to remain with that identity, you're a cisgender woman.

Transgender

It's an umbrella term for people who transition through medical assistance from their birth sex to their desired sex. They're more than just the trans men and trans women but include non-binary or gender queer. On a broad scale, transgender people can be called cross-dressers.

Bigender

Bigender is a term relating to a person who has a combination of two genders. They have just two genders, masculine and feminine.

Omnigender

This refers to seeing all genders as the same and not discriminating against one from the other. An omnigender person can possess only one gender but can easily pass it off for another.

Agender

People under this identity are indifferent toward identifying with any gender. At times, they do not have any gender at all. Agender can also be called genderless, neutral gender, null-gender, or neutrinos. Androgyne is a synonymous word that is slightly different from the other words. It is a mixture of masculinity and femininity, and they have the characteristics of both a man and a woman's behaviors.

Butch

This is a term used in lesbianism. It's associated with a lesbian who expresses more masculinity. Femme is the opposite of Butch. A lesbian who represents more femininity is called a femme. Butch can be said as a type of gender identity, as most homosexuals are familiar with this.

Gender Expansive

It's an umbrella term recognized by the LGBTQIA for persons who choose to push past definitions of gender held by their culture. They express their sexuality outside of what their culture would expect. Transgender people are part of gender-expansive.

Genderfluid

A person who identifies as genderfluid doesn't have a fixed expression of their identity. The person could feel masculine in a particular place at a specific time, but when they leave that environment, his identity changes to feminine, like a fluctuation.

Gender Outlaw

Like a fish out of water, a gender outlaw refuses to let society's definition of masculinity and femininity define them.

Genderqueer

Also called non-binary, genderqueer persons refuse to identify as either male or female. They do not classify under the gender binary but fit more under the transgender umbrella, although some genderqueer persons do not consider themselves transgender.

Masculine of Center

Let's call it boyishness. In the LGBTQ community, masculine of center (MOC) persons are lesbians or trans or bend more towards the masculinity line.

Polygender and Pangender

Persons in this identity group have multiple gender identities.

■■

HOW SEXUALITY AFFECTS SPIRITUALITY

IS THERE A POSSIBILITY?

When I first came across this topic many years ago as a teenager, I was utterly perplexed and raised my eyebrows in wonder and confusion about how these concepts were connected. As an adult with many years of sexual and spiritual experience who's here to guide you, it gives me so much pleasure that I'm writing about this. I can't help but let a small smile creep up my lips because the concepts are entirely on fire.

Years ago, I made friends with a woman called Kira. We hardly see each other anymore because she moved recently after getting married, but I place a call to check up on her whenever I can. She does so, too. It's a mutual friendship.

When we first became friends, we listened to a podcast on spirituality that got us talking on a particular day, and I can still remember her words. "It's either sex or spirituality. They don't align."

I knew little about spirituality and sexuality back then, so I couldn't hold a solid argument. Kira had been brainwashed with the false narrative that she had to choose between sex and pursuing her spiritual life, and somehow she managed to convince me too. But it was only for a short while because I didn't believe in a thing such as spirituality. Now that I think about it, it's funny how convicted she was, and it's sad because, for a great deal of her life, she stuck to the spiritual part because, according to her, whenever she tried to merge both, they always repelled, like both sides of a magnet.

When I took a course on sexuality and spirituality, I learned that I needed affirmation—something to remind me that sexuality and spirituality went hand in hand. I went back to Kira and asked if she was still convicted. This time, her reply was utterly different.

She had switched from spirituality to sexuality, and while that was okay, she was still unable to handle both. She had sex with whoever she wanted, and it didn't matter to her anymore. I went back home and sat down to evaluate what struck me.

I thought about it that even religions are not against sex. Most care about not doing it outside of marriage because they consider it sacred. Spirituality, more than religiosity, is simply about transcending beyond your physical self and aligning with your spiritual self, your divine. So I said that if I feel entirely at peace with myself and have the values central to sexuality and spirituality, who says practicing sexuality and spirituality is impossible?

As humans, we've all been influenced by society, religious beliefs, our families, or cultural beliefs, whatever it is. Significantly growing up as kids, we had watched our family members or people around us carry out specific actions and express ideas in specific things or practices. Children like to mimic a lot, and it's a primary reason we're who we are today, having values differing slightly or entirely from one another. Some women grew up being told by their parents or guardians that sex was sinful. They told them these lies to prevent them from having sex, but it usually proved abortive because most of these women later grew up to realize these lies and defied them.

But again, all homes are different in their way. Some homes celebrate sex and encourage their children to engage in it with someone special. It all boils down to your attitudes towards things around you, sex inclusive, which your spiritual belief can guide.

How Spirituality Can Influence A Woman

Sexuality and spirituality are very powerful forces, and both can help us understand the complexity and mystery of the world we find ourselves in.

Spirituality can influence a woman in more than one way, but I'd like us to focus on the aspect of sexuality. Spirituality comes with moral values which you're to abide by to live a fulfilling, spiritual life, agreed? When you decide to live a spiritual life, there are many things you might have to set aside to commune with your divine faith. I hope you're getting it? Now sex in its entirety is more than the physical, and these values you now abide by as a result of your sexuality are a part of your sexual experience.

Spirituality can influence a woman who has sex randomly and without a condom. It can influence whether or not to have sex with just anyone, whether or not to use birth control, and even how we handle our relationships. So engaging in sexual activities that contradict the values you abide by will certainly affect your health.

For instance, your spiritual values could be a commitment to one sexual partner, being honest, loyal, etcetera. The moment you step outside that circle and do otherwise, you've created a gap, and negative emotions will set in. You could have feelings of guilt, fear, and self-loathe. This is how spirituality can influence you as a woman.

It is important to understand the values of spirituality and practice them faithfully. Also, note that our faith can change over time, likewise becoming stronger as we grow older.

Sexuality and Spirituality; One Side of a Coin?

I'm about to discuss sexuality and how it affects spirituality, but I need to bring back some definitions to make things easier. In chapter one of this book, I talked about spirituality being "the search for one's inner wealth," seeking "a meaningful connection with something beyond the physical, which causes positive emotions such as peace, contentment, gratitude, and acceptance." Spirituality is about deciding to transcend above our physical self and keying into our spiritual self, our true form that is keen on nothing but positivity. I've talked a lot about spirituality with you and why you need to embrace your spirituality as a black woman to be the best version of yourselves, to allow love to come in, not just to ourselves alone but to others.

Now I'm going to introduce sexuality, which I'm guessing you know pretty much a lot about after my last talk on it. By the way, how's it going with knowing your sexuality, my beautiful black woman? Have you stopped being confused about who you are, and you're like, "you know what? F*ck it. This is who I am, it's something I've always been, or I'm getting into terms with, and as long as it makes me happy, as long as it makes me feel alive, I'm going to keep being me no matter what."

If you've declared such positivity over your life, I am immensely happy for you, and I can't wait to see you move mountains. Also, if you're still on a journey to finding your sexuality, I want you to know that I have gone through such a stage, I've seen and walked a lot of people through this stage, and while it can be daunting and all confusing, it's only worth celebrating that you decided to at least try. So here's to all strong black women searching for their sexuality. I applaud you, I appreciate you and understand your situation, and I want you to know that you're not alone in this. You're never alone, and all you need is time for things to fall in place by themselves. You've got this, black queen!

I defined sexuality as one of the fundamental forces behind people's thoughts, behaviors, and feelings. It encompasses how procreation occurs and talks about one's psychological and sociological beliefs about sex. Sexuality is regulated by various parts of the brain, which shape the body and mind towards seeking pleasure. I want to state that the entirety of sexuality is about sex, sexual orientation, reproduction, gender identity, and pleasure, and we'll be focusing a bit more on sex in this chapter. I hope you've got your pen ready? Let's jump in!

How Have You Been Having Sex?

A lot, and I mean a whole lot, has been said about the word sex. Different views of sex are flying all over the net, with some viewing it as sacred, and I don't mean it religiously. More like in a way that it is special between partners indulging in it. Most religions proclaim sex outside of marriage as sin, while others view sex as natural and a thing to be celebrated. What do I view sex as?

I think sex is sacred, and that's why I'm even talking about the connection between sexuality and spirituality in the first place. Whatever your view of sex is, even the unmentioned ones in this text, is perfectly okay by me as long as you're fine with it. Either way, we still get to learn about sexuality and spirituality.

Despite all that has been said about sex, with more focus on the negative part, it is key to understand that sex is not going anywhere. Oh yes, it is an essential function of humanity. It's a generally known fact that sex has tons of health benefits. Lowering blood pressure, reducing the likelihood of prostate cancer, and improving cardiovascular health are a few benefits. Sex is physical and spiritual, and before you say, "who the hell is this guy talking about sex being spiritual?" Stay with me a while as I explain what I mean.

Remember me saying spirituality is getting in tune with our inner being? However, did you know that sex is a universal force, not just a force but an immense one? You have sex with a partner for the sake of love, or just casual sex that you may think doesn't mean anything. But what if it did?

It's not just about the moans and all the pleasure you feel at that moment. There's a totality in it. As you touch your partner's body, you touch their mind and heart, and more often not, these sexual intercourses leave lasting impressions on your innermost selves. Let me break it down.

If you've had sex, this illustration should be easy to understand.

Have you ever been in a position where after intercourse with your partner, you feel at peace and somewhat joyful, like you're on top of the world? You feel like your spirits are connected, and it's not just about you anymore. You're constantly looking for ways to make your partner happy in several ways. Or maybe not. Maybe none of these happen, and you feel a completely different way. You've not linked your sexuality to your spirituality, and here, my beautiful black queen, is where the link between sexuality and spirituality comes in.

The Link Between Sexuality And Spirituality

Spirituality is about discovering who you truly are — looking into your inner being where there's purity and sexuality is a vital part of it.

During or after spiritual sex, you feel loved and content and, like I said, at peace with your being. A woman who's at peace with herself will willingly contribute to the welfare of others. Most times, people at peace and content with themselves care less about the vain things of life like going after power and fame, material possessions, etc.; all they wish to do is to keep basking in the freedom they've found for themselves while spreading values like love, humility, compassion, and respect.

Woody Harrelson said, "When I was in my twenties and just so sexually prolific, the first time I went to Machu Picchu, this guy, a spiritual teacher, says to me, "When you make love, you must be making love." I thought that was the greatest advice I had ever heard." The link between sexuality and spirituality is the concepts is orgasm, sex, and love. Like what the spiritual teacher said about making love, it's truly important not just to have sex with someone random, but with a partner you're sure is the one for you. A partner you genuinely love and are certain that the feeling is mutual. That way, you're able to make love, and on getting to orgasm, you harness the full potential of your sexual energy.

When I talk about sexuality and spirituality, I do not mean the casual sex that many people in this generation indulge in. Don't get me wrong; I'm not condemning anyone. Whatever you feel is best for you, I'm solidly behind you that you go for it as long as you're not hurting anyone. But I wish to clear your mind that sexuality and spirituality can only be linked when there's love and orgasm, and I don't mean some orgasm you reach through a stranger or someone you don't love, but with someone you don't love.

Having spiritual sex with someone you truly love can positively affect your relationship and cause you both to become more intimate and connected.

Spiritual Women and Sex

I didn't forget we're talking about women, so the focus is on you now. From research, I found out that spirituality has greater consequences among young adults, especially women – than religion. Due to the topic, I went on to study research at a University here in the US and got to interview up to a hundred students, more than half of which were women. I asked them about their thoughts on spirituality, and surprisingly, most of them knew and took their spirituality seriously. The ones who did acknowledge that it helps them experience this sense of fulfillment and somehow connects them emotionally to all of humanity.

"If we want the world to be a better place, let's all get in tune with our spirituality." One of the women had started, and it struck a chord.

As for the males and their responses, the majority of the males didn't see a link between sexuality and spirituality, and genuinely, it's harder for men to see sexuality as spiritual because that's how they're built. A woman can crave intimacy with her partner, and all a man would be thinking of is how to climax and get the urge out of him. He can do this with anyone and not feel attached to his partners, but it's a lot harder for women, hence why it's easier for women to accept that there's a thing as spiritual sex.

Studies show that practicing yoga and other physical activities that promote mental fitness have helped many women who were formally sexually unsatisfied experience a greater level of arousal and orgasms. Spiritual women may also feel comfortable having many sex partners and not see the need to use a condom.

A lingering question might be bugging you at the back of your mind, just like it did years ago. Is it spirituality that makes women want more sex?

Good thing I now have an answer for that.

Scientists have revealed that physical exercises and meditation can set you on a path to bliss, and orgasms help in the effective relief against body pains. Hence, the desire for sex among those connected to the spiritual part of themselves. Having deep conversations about sex with your partner and just talking about ways of improving your sex life can profoundly affect your relationship. So spirituality in itself can spur a woman to want more sex since it connects her to your divine and her partner every time you do.

Using Your Sexuality to Attain Spirituality

As we converse, dear beautiful black woman, we'll be engaging in some practicals, most of which would require you to imagine. Cool, isn't it?

I need you to imagine yourself with your partner and in the mood for sex. They are caressing you and making you feel completely loved and in the spotlight with every touch of theirs. There's so much spark or sexual energy in you, and you feel yourself experiencing pleasure and an emotional connection to your partner. Every detailed touch they give strengthens these feelings, and all you can feel is the unification of your body, mind, and spirit with your partner. Take your imagination up and focus on the period of orgasm, where everything seems timeless, and it's like you've lost yourself in your partner.

Orgasm is got from a French word, 'Orgasmós,' which means 'excitement' and 'swelling.' The French call it 'La petite mort,' which translates to "the little death." Wikipedia says this expression means "the brief loss or weakening of consciousness." During orgasm, a woman loses consciousness for a brief moment and transcends to a state of bliss where she doesn't have to worry about anything.

Now tell me, during your orgasm, did you think about the bills you haven't paid? Or the debtor who's yet to pay?

I don't know about you, but I don't think about my problems. All I can feel is unity with myself, my partner, and the universe. That feeling is what it means to be awakened spiritually. I know these feelings can be short-lived but picture and view them as enlightenments of what being connected to the universe can truly feel like.

When I say using your sexuality to attain your spirituality, I'm talking about viewing sex as something other than a mere physical interaction, like a spiritual practice, like the yoga and meditation exercises you do. If you want to be connected to your partner and feel like one with him, then I'll sexual spirituality is the most effective way.

One time, I had so many bills, all coming after the other, piling up and causing my blood pressure to rise. My cousin was sick, and all I could do was worry about him. My partner came over and saw me in that state. She smiled, and the next thing she did was place her lips on mine. She kissed me and told me that sex helped to reduce stress. I found it funny because I knew that, but up till that moment, I had doubts about it.

As I made love to her, I could feel all the pressure and thoughts evaporating, and I was instantly in nirvana when I experienced orgasm.

Sex can take you to beautiful places you've only imagined. It gives you the feeling that nothing is wrong and happiness rests within your human form and lifetime.

Some women have no personal idea of sex. All they wish to do is satisfy their partners to make the relationship work, no matter what it costs them. You can call them partner pleasers. Haha! It's a term I coined by myself. They're afraid of rocking the boat and would rather see themselves drown in the sea of frustration and dissatisfaction. I wish you to deal with this and get past these terrible feelings. Understand that sex isn't something you need to give others without you benefiting from it. Take time to learn about what you want and what your body desires, and commit to sexual encounters to boost morale and connect you to yourself and your partner.

You automatically reconnect to the divine or universe as you connect to yourself and your partner. When the parties involved intentionally connect to their spirituality, then sex becomes something more than physical activity.

This, my beautiful black woman, is what spiritual sex is about.

Sex As a Physical Activity And Spiritual Practice

You may be wondering what the difference is. Isn't sex just sex? The truth is that sex can be whatever you see it as. I choose to see it as a spiritual practice. It doesn't mean others see it that way, but as a woman on her journey to spirituality, I advise that you navigate your belief into seeing sex as a spiritual practice.

What is the difference?

The difference between physical and spiritual sex lies in whether it is casual or conscious.

An instance would be when you easily vibe to the lyrics of one of the songs of your favorite artist anytime it comes up on the radio. Fine, you know it verbatim, but that's where it ends. You don't make an effort to stream or download the song, but you can openly brag that it's your favorite song. Another instance is when you stream the music, save up to attend live performances by your favorite artist, and stay updated with their lifestyle.

These examples perfectly describe how casual sex and conscious sex are different. You can guess correctly that the first instance is what casual sex is about, while the second is about mindful sex.

In our world today, many people prefer to engage in casual sex because why not? It's less stressful, there are no commitments, and you don't have to feel the headache that comes with giving your all, but in the end, there remains a void that only conscious sex can fill.

Conscious sex provides for intimacy, and when everything is correct, you get to feel complete and at peace, and eventually, casual sex will no longer appeal to you. Who wants to listen to music on the radio when it can stream the song and be comfortable?

A wiki definition of casual sex is any "sexual activity outside a romantic relationship and implies an absence of commitment, emotional attachment, or familiarity between sexual partners." People who engage in casual sex only focus on getting their desires met, either physical or emotional.

Conscious sex, on the other hand, is about creating a connection with your partner to reconnect your body, mind, and spirit to the divine. After sex, it's no longer about you but your connection to someone else and the universe. This spirituality gives sex a whole new meaning.

How To Get In Tune With Your Spirituality Through Sex

To do this, you would need to drop that casual sex and pick up the art of conscious sex. Let's go, black queen!

Be Certain

First things first, ask yourself specific questions. Are you ready to become connected to someone? Will you be comfortable talking about your desires and needs and listening to your partner?

I know how much I've said that sex is more than a physical experience for me, and, to be honest, this repetition is essential. Sex connects you to your partner and is not a sport or something to jump into because you're horny. It'll be better to engage in self-love rather than have casual sex and desire spirituality where you do not have to gamble with someone else's emotions. So my beautiful black woman, be sure that you're ready to have a part of someone in you and a part of you in someone before letting them in.

Also, you do not have to let the propaganda about sex get to you. You do not have to feel ashamed for having sex. It's a beautiful, wonderful experience that should be consensual and free.

Mutual Affection

Sex would be lacking if you or your partner went into it for self-gratification. Spiritual sex should include both partners being intentional and deciding to make the experience worthwhile.

Take away all distractions and communicate with your partner to make sure they're finding the experience pleasurable just as you are. Make sure they're comfortable, and just as you're doing this, they should return the same energy. Sex would be great if we all showed mutual affection to our partners, and we would get in touch with our spirituality that way.

You're Both Divine Manifestations of God

Don't forget spirituality is keying into your inner being and connecting your body, mind, and spirit with the divine. Once you're spiritual, you become a divine manifestation, so I encourage you to view them as such when considering who to choose as a sex partner. Just as you are a divine manifestation of a higher force, so is your partner.

Strive to understand and not judge them. Sex is like a worship of the divine. Your partner with whom you have sex represents the divine, and by connecting your spirit to them, you connect to the divine.

Meditation

As you have sex, it's important not to drift out of the moment. Try as much as you can to focus your attention on your body and observe the sensations you feel.

Consider sex as a meditation. Rather than putting all your effort into achieving orgasm, why not focus on the pleasure you give and receive?

It's essential to experiment with your bodies. Communicate about what turns you on and if you feel your mind drifting away, remember to bring back your focus.

Motive

Before having sex, be sure of your motives and your partner's. If you have different reasons, it won't lead to spirituality. For instance, if one of you wants to have sex for fun while the other wishes for something more, you can make the best bet what's going to happen to the relationship.

I'd love you to understand that you can have casual sex with someone you love and conscious sex with someone you just met. It all boils down to your intention. What do you want? Do you desire to have a spiritual experience through sex? Then it's best to be intentional about it.

If you're going to have sex for fun, talk it out with your partner. If you're genuinely hoping it'll lead to the start of something great, communicate.

Expectations

Ask yourself how you would like this experience to end. Then ask your partner. Do you both share the exact expectations?

Make sure you still feel the same way you felt initially and do not want to run away after sex. That may just be a sign that you're having casual sex.

Twelve Months Transformation Journal

Finally, we've come to the last segment of your journey, but I'd like to urge you not to feel pressured to start this transformation journal with me until you're ready because it will take commitment and zeal to go through with it every day. Don't forget that it transcends beyond that. Spirituality is a part of living, and this is just a guideline to help you walk that part for as long as you please. I'm sure that it would have become a lifestyle before these fifty-two weeks elapsed.

I've made this journal into a weekly journal to make things easier for you. Each week has seven different activities you're to do every day for us to make significant progress. Don't forget to make the most of this journal. Make it your companion and mentor.

One last thing – have fun!

Week One: Meeting With Your Spirituality

Activity One – It Is Your Journey Alone

Make it a mission today to understand and always remember that this is a journey of self-discovery; hence only you can truly discover yourself.

Choosing to be like someone is okay, but it's essential not to neglect your true capabilities.

Activity Two – Find A Watchword

So your second activity for the week is to find a watchword that you can stick to. It could be a phrase, slogan, or even a quote, anything at all.

Pasting it on your board is a tip to help you remember it faster.

Activity Three – Affirmations

Declare positivity in your life. You're a goal-getter, beautiful, and on a journey to self-discovery and will come out a badass, you know, words like these. Hype yourself always, black queen.

Activity Four – Meditate

Take out about fifteen minutes for yourself and meditate. Chanting or mindfulness can also help calm your mind. Don't forget to do this daily.

Activity Five – Exercise

Your mind alone shouldn't be the only part of you at peace. Let your body feel powerful. Do exercises, yoga, drum, sing, dance even!

Activity Six – Laugh It Out

Laughter, they say, is the best medicine, and I subscribe to that. Don't be so uptight always. If something silly or embarrassing happens, laugh it out. It brings joy.

Activity Seven – Go Over The Activities

I'd love to know what watchword you found.

What were the words you declared about yourself?

How did the meditation go?

I hope you had fun while exercising? If you haven't exercised for a while, you'll need some time to adjust, but you'll be fine.

Laugh!

Week Two: Feeding Your Mind

Activity One – Read A Book

Your guess was right; that was the first thing I would say. Yes, spend at least thirty minutes of your time reading daily.

Activity Two – Listen To A Podcast

Listening to podcasts while exercising, walking, or doing random things will tremendously enrich your mind.

Activity Three – Watch A Documentary

Have you tried Netflix or Amazon Prime documentaries if you find the regular documentary boring? Spiced! Remember, feed your mind.

Activity Four – Question Your Beliefs

You could start by questioning what you were taught in childhood. When you ask questions, you become curious for answers. In finding solutions, you'll be sure to get some new knowledge.

Activity Five – Games

If you're a gamer, I suggest including brain teasers in your collection. I think they're great for developing your brain.

Activity Six – Stop The Comparison

You're only hurting yourself by comparing yourself to others. Experience genuine authenticity and self-love when you stop the comparison.

Activity Seven – Connect With Like-Minded People

If you wish, join a book club, go-to hangout spots, and relax with people who think like you. It's refreshing.

Week Three: Trying Something New

Activity One – Make a list.

Write out a list of things you'd love to do, learn, places you'd love to visit, and people you'd love to meet. Make a neat list.

Activity Two – Make A Choice

It's time to arrange your list in the order of priority and choose which one to begin with.

Activity Three – Find Out The Obstacles

Determine what the obstacles to achieving these goals would be. Time, money, fear, etc

Activity Four – Draft A Plan

Make a plan on how you can overcome these obstacles. You could save up some money, create time out of your schedule, and be determined. Setting deadlines can help a great deal, but if it would make you feel pressured, I'd instead you don't.

Activity Five – Seek Support

If it would make you feel better to talk to someone about your plan, go for it. Surround yourself with people who would readily support your dreams.

Activity Six-Step Out!

Take that action now. Visit that place, that person. Do what you've always wanted. Step out of your shell.

Activity Seven – Celebrate That Milestone

A round of applause for you on achieving such a feat! You're genuinely a black woman. No matter how little, I truly celebrate you. It would help if you did so too.

Week Four: Achieving Positivity

Activity One – Identify That Negativity

Observe yourself and pick out where you're primarily negative. Now, ask your close friends or spouse about a negative aspect of your life. This part might surprise you.

Activity Two – Find The Root Of Your Negativity

Now that you know the negative aspects of yourself. It's time to deal with the root cause. Take some time to think about what you think could be the cause, then go ahead to tackle it.

Activity Three – Focus On The Good Part

When you're done tackling the negativity, we can now work on achieving positivity. Repeat the same process in activity one and find out yourself. Ask your friends or spouse.

Activity Four – Express Gratitude

Make a list of one thing you're grateful for every day. It enhances awareness of self and things surrounding you.

Activity Five – Laugh And Laugh Again

I will recommend this in many activities for different weeks because I can't stress the importance enough. Even when you don't feel like it, attempt to laugh. It gets easier with time.

Activity Six – Take It Easy

Take it easy on yourself. Try not to let your anger out on yourself when things infuriate or sadden you by self-inflicting damage or harsh words.

Activity Seven – Seek Professional Help

If you don't see progress in your journey to positivity and feel there's a lot more, I urge you to seek professional help as soon as you can. You'd feel much better.

Week Five: Embracing Nature

Activity One – Understand Nature And How It Affects You

I might have to talk about this extensively someday, but you have to do your research for now. Understand how essential nature is to you if you're to find this week interesting.

Activity Two – Narrow The Question To Yourself

When you research, you will find things about the beauty of nature. Now it's time to ask yourself what you love about nature. You don't have to force things; go slowly.

Activity Three – Find Your Nature Spot

It would help a great deal to find a great place in nature where you can meditate or exercise. It doesn't have to be so far away. And no, I'm not giving any suggestions. I'm leaving you to figure this out by yourself, beautiful queen.

Activity Four – Make It A Habit

If you haven't been doing so much in nature, you will have to challenge yourself to develop the habit. Relaxing outside, eating outside, gardening, anything to can think of.

Activity Five – It's The Quality That Matters

It's usually not about how long you spend being in nature but the quality. It wouldn't make sense that you're essential with your mind joggled up with many thoughts. Be in nature and feel at peace.

Activity Six – Sticky Notes

I said sticky notes, and we know what they mean, reminders. If you have a busy schedule, you can place a sticky note on your refrigerator or anywhere you quickly go. Also, your phones can help too.

Activity Seven – Relax

Has it been one hell of a week? It's time to do nothing but relax in nature. Go for an outdoor retreat, step out in the morning, and hang out with a nature buddy. Just relax.

Week Six: Feeding Your Body

Activity One – Always Eat Breakfast

Most people skip breakfast because they're busy or think it helps them lose weight, but you need a breakfast rich in high fiber and low in sugar, fat, and salt for a balanced diet. You can research healthy breakfast ideas and map out a food timetable to follow.

Activity Two – Drink Water

Health experts recommend that you drink a lot of water daily with an average of 8 glasses which should equal 2 liters of water. Never let yourself get dehydrated.

Activity Three – Eat Lots Of Fruits And Veggies

It is recommended that you eat lots of fruits every day. Make it a duty to eat at least five portions of a type of fruit. Also, don't forget to include vegetables in your food.

Activity Four – Eat More Fish

Fish gives protein, a necessary food class, and is needed for a healthy balanced diet. You're also advised to eat oily fish as it contains omega-3 fats, which are suitable for helping to prevent heart disease.

Activity Five – Use Less Salt

Excess salt intake can increase your heart blood pressure, leading to heart disease or even stroke. So as you cook and eat, pls try to make use of less salt.

Activity Six – Reduce Your Saturated Fat And Sugar Intake

Excess saturated fat increases the amount of cholesterol in your blood system, which can also cause heart disease. Reduced saturated fat intake means cutting down on foods like butter, hard cheese, cakes, etc.

Also, note today that excess sugar can increase your risk of tooth decay and obesity.

Activity Seven – Exercise

Lastly, I'd love for you to begin exercising daily for this week. No matter how fit you think you are, exercising, just like eating healthy foods, can help reduce the risk of obesity and other diseases, especially heart diseases.

Week Seven: Practicing Gratitude

Activity One – Understand Why You Should Practice Gratitude

I do not wish to impose my beliefs on you, so it's only proper that I enlighten you on why you should practice gratitude.

Gratitude significantly boosts happiness, helps you feel more positive emotions, and improves your relationship with others, among a host of other benefits. So I'll implore you to do your research and decide to embark on this journey to practice gratitude or not.

Activity Two – Have A Journal

I expect that by now, you have a journal you're working with for your spirituality. Another separate journal, however, is also a good idea in your journey to expressing gratitude.

Activity Three – Be Specific About What You're Grateful For

I'd like you not just to express gratitude but to be particular about your expression. If you're thankful for something, write it down. For example: "I'm thankful that I am in this situation today," or "I am thankful that I made a lot of progress in my work today."

Activity Four – Go Into Detail

Saying something isn't usually enough. To practice gratitude, you should explain what you are grateful for and why you are. You don't feel like it's an obligation to express gratitude.

Activity Five – Don't Ignore The Negative.

When your life is going so well, don't forget the times when things were rough because it is in that forgetfulness that pride sets in. Remembering how you came to a certain level would help you express gratitude.

Activity Six – Use Reminders

At times you may tend to forget about what you've achieved or what someone has done for you and not express gratitude when you should. Using visual reminders and asking yourself questions like "What has this person given to me?" "Have I achieved a goal I should be grateful for?" etc., would help a great deal.

Activity Seven – Express Gratitude Outwardly

Once you've been grateful inwardly, like expressing gratitude in your journal and all of that, you're ready for the outside world. Use words like "Thank you," "I appreciate what you've done for me," etc., to build stronger relationships with people.

Week Eight: Voicing Out Affirmations

This week will be a bit different from the rest because the entire week will be about affirmations on various subjects. I'll list out three but feel free to add as much as you desire!

Activity One – Affirmations For Health

"I am grateful for my body."

"Whatever I feel in my body, I will tend to it with utmost care and precision, never judging or being hard on my body."

"I am open to new ways of living a healthy lifestyle."

Activity Two – Affirmations For Love

"I let go of every negativity that came with my past love, and I am willing to receive a new love."

"I am ready to stay committed to nurturing the heart."

"I deserve all the love I'm being showered because I return just as much."

Activity Three – Affirmations For Self-Esteem

"I deserve to get everything I desire."

"I will soar above the sky and achieve all my goals."

"I am a brilliant woman and the most beautiful."

Activity Four – Affirmations For Self-Love

"I choose not to give in to stress and self-harm."

"Whenever I feel stressed, I'll always remember to pause and take a deep breath."

"No one is perfect. I acknowledge my mistake and admit my flaws. However, I'm not letting it get to me. I will try again."

Activity Five – Affirmations For Peace And Harmony

"I've begun my spiritual journey and will strive to attain inner peace."

"I have a good relationship with my friends and family. I love them, and they love me."

"Everything is in perfect control."

Activity Six – Affirmations For Joy And Happiness

"Everything right now is working for my good."

"I am a happy woman."

"I am full of joy and happiness; therefore, I will live longer."

Activity Seven – Affirmations For Anxiety

"Everything seems as though it's tumbling, but I choose to be calm."
"Things eventually turn out to be okay in the end. I have to take a deep breath."

"I'm overthinking right now. I should stop it."

Week Nine: Finding Peace Amidst Chaos

Activity One - Get Occupied

It doesn't necessarily mean working or doing something strenuous, watching your favorite tv shows, drawing, dancing, engaging in karaoke, hanging out, etc. Any fun thing you love to do to distract you.

Activity Two – Stop Consuming Negativity

Some people tend to self-destruct when they're faced with challenges. If social media is the primary source of negativity in your life, it's better to take a break. Walk away from anything that doubles your sadness.

Activity Three – Get Rid Of The Stress

If you're feeling stressed, you could take a walk, jog, go on a vacation, exercise, or any other idea you have of ridding of stress.

Activity Four – Refine Your Brain With Positive Affirmation

Remember last week; I gave some affirmations about peace and anxiety. Claims of peace should help you control your emotions.

Activity Five – Stop Doubting

If you approach a situation with doubt in your mind, there's a high chance that you aren't going to make the best of it. So whatever you're going through, you have to approach it with courage and hope that things will fall into place.

Activity Six – Focus On Your Purpose

Things are tough right now, but you have a goal to achieve and a purpose of fulfilling. It wouldn't be right for you to give up. Take a break, find calm in that raging storm but don't give up.

Activity Seven – Seek Help

It could be your problem is beyond all of these solutions, but this last one should do the trick. Talk to someone, a friend, family, or professional. Let them know what you're going through and seek advice from them.

Week Ten: Read A Book

Activity One – Decide

Before buying your book, you have to skim through the contents and decide which book you will read for the entire week. Then make that purchase.

Activity Two – Reason For Choice

What made you decide to get that particular book? Can you write what intrigues you most about the text in your journal? I'd also love to hear it if you can.

Activity Three – Jot Down As You Read

Jotting down can help you remember points you've learned from the book. Also, jotting down new words would help expand your vocabulary and keep you abreast with ideologies.

Activity Four – Relax Your Mind

Don't feel pressured to read if you don't feel like it. Make sure you're calm and begin reading if you're to get value from the book you're reading effectively.

Activity Five: Put Into Practice What You've Learnt.

Remember the words you jotted down? It's time to reread them. Try to use those new words in your everyday conversations. Also, the moral lessons you've learned should be put into practice.

Activity Six – Finding A Reading Partner

At times you may feel alone when you start reading a book. Finding someone who finds interest in reading will help a great deal in boosting your interests. Your partner can cheer you up when the need arises and recommend great books for you.

Activity Seven – Join A Book Club

Book clubs are great places to go to broaden your knowledge of books and spike up your interests.

Week Eleven: Adopting The Virtue Of Forgiveness

Activity One – Accept That Everyone Makes Mistakes.

This is one of the first steps taken to forgiveness. Realizing that no one is above mistakes makes you understand that you can make mistakes too and will want to be forgiven. This should make forgiveness relatively easy for you.

Activity Two – Mistakes Are A Part Of Life

No matter how we try to shy away from the truth, the reality will always be that mistakes are s part of life and will frame whatever we might become in the future, depending on how we take it.

Activity Three – Don't hold Grudges.

Have you been offended by anyone? No matter who that person may be, let them know that they have crossed a line they shouldn't have. Please don't keep it to yourself.

Activity Four – Forgive Others

The gravity of an offense could make this very hard to do. But it'll be the best decision you will ever make. The freedom that comes with forgiveness is limitless.

Activity Five – Forgive Yourself.

You probably have done something that you weren't proud of in the distant past and recent past. You've got to let go of yourself too. It's not the end of the world.

Activity Six – Make Amends

If you're not making progress from your mistakes, you're making a more significant mistake, and that's not the woman you are. Make amends and grow stronger every day.

Activity Seven – Affirmation

I have mistakes too, and as I forgive myself, I will also ignore the people around me who have offended me. That's how I want to live my life.

Week Twelve: Adopting the Virtue of Prudence

Activity One – Understanding Prudence

Prudence is the virtue of being careful about the choices you make. Stopping to think about your next move and not taking unnecessary risks. It is a virtue of careful thinking for better decision-making.

Activity Two - Understanding The Need To Be Prudent

Why should you be prudent? The life you see can happen to anyone at any time. You wouldn't want to overlook that because one careless decision can cost you more than you can even imagine.

Activity Three – Counsel Yourself

Taking any crucial decision in your life requires you to brainstorm extensively. Don't ever rush to make decisions you might regret later. Making decisions on impulse could be fatal.

Activity Four – Seek Counsel From Others

You're not alone in the world. If you feel that you're at crossroads and don't know what to do, seek help from those you think are capable of helping you.

Activity Five – Learn From Your Past

You have made mistakes in the past and gained knowledge in the process. Use that knowledge when the need arises so that you don't make the same mistake twice.

Activity Six – Weighing Your Risks and Rewards.

To make decisions carefully, weighing your risks and rewards can be a handy tool. Ask yourself, this risk I am about to take, is it worth the reward? The answer to that question can shape your thought process and enable you to make good decisions.

Activity Seven – You Are Responsible For The Consequences Of Your Actions

Whenever you want to make a decision, always remember that you will be held liable for whatever action you take after you have made your decision.

Week Thirteen – Adopting The Virtue Of Temperance

Activity One - Understanding The Virtue Of Temperance

This, in simpler terms, is a virtue of restraint, and it is based on particularly whatever an individual seeks to refrain from doing. It could be alcoholism, extravagant spending, or whatever vice an individual deems not worthy of doing.

Activity Two – Identifying Toxic Traits

Identifying those things you want to refrain from is a start of a good foot to abstaining from them. If you don't know what you want, you can hardly achieve anything.

Activity Three - Acknowledging Your Toxic Traits

This may look like the previous subtopic, but a thin line differentiates them. It's not healthy to deceive yourself. When you know that you have a toxic trait, say, alcoholism, you shouldn't lie to yourself about it.

By acknowledging your condition, you make it easy to make efforts to refrain.

Activity Four – Have Them Written Down

This is a very underrated activity. Get a journal just like this, one; of the things you wish to refrain from; go through them at the start of your day to remind yourself and see how well you fared at the end of the day.

Activity Five – Monitor Your Progress

From time to time, look back at how you've been faring. How have things changed? How often did you go clubbing and get wasted? When was the last time you rolled a joint? Question yourself about the journey.

Activity Six – Celebrate Your Progress

Commend yourself for a job well done with each step you take up the ladder to Temperance. This doesn't mean you should throw a party or something. It is something that happens from within. Even a smile of satisfaction would do.

Activity Seven – Don't Be So Hard on Yourself.

The journey would not be a linear one. One after the other. No-no-no. You'll fall back sometimes, but you always have to stay calm and not be hard on yourself. You're human.

Week Fourteen – Adopting The Virtue Of Justice

Activity One – Understanding The Virtue of Justice

In human relations, justice means giving each person what they deserve. Not treating everyone the same, but treating them accordingly. It would help if you understood that equality is not justice.

Activity Two – Applying Justice To Your Self Improvement

This virtue may not only pertain to your relationship with humans. You can apply justice to your personal life. This means things that you do that are important to you. It could be education, a craft, your work, workouts, and many others.

Activity Three – Knowing How To Do Justice To Your Everyday Living.

The previous chapter spoke about justice being applied to other spheres of life. Here is a simple formula to help you streamline your activities so that you'd be doing justice to them; Focus your attention on the things you know will benefit you in the long run. They are deserving of your attention, and that's what justice entails.

Activity Four – Knowing How To Do Justice To People

This should be simple. Go all out for the people that do the same for you. Make time for the people that do the same for you. There's no time trying to impress who wouldn't even care. Show love to those that are deserving of it.

Activity Five – Studying How You Relate With People

Have you closely watched how you relate with people wherever you go? Church, School, Workplace? What are the patterns that you have noticed? Could you take note of them?

Activity Six – Study The Patterns

The patterns that you have noticed, you have to study them to decipher the loopholes. Are you treating people based on their race, gender, financial status, or political power? That would be unfair to them. On the other hand, are you giving too much attention to those who care about you and neglecting those who do? That'll be unfair to yourself.

Activity Seven – Work On Improvement

What's a study without usage? You know what ought to be and ought not. So make use of that knowledge from studying the patterns to improve yourself.

Week Fifteen – Adopting The Virtue Of Fortitude

Activity One – Understanding The Virtue of Fortitude

One of the visible traits of a black woman is Fortitude. It means that one manages to be solid or courageous even amid adversity and pain.

Activity Two – Understanding That Life Is Full Of Challenges

Even for the children born into wealthy homes, life would still be full of challenges. No man has lived an entirely peaceful life till he died. If you don't understand that, you should now.

Activity Three – Understanding The Need To Have Fortitude

Some may be asking, why do I need to show strength while passing through adversity? If you're one of those, don't forget to ask yourself who'd be willing to associate with a weak person. Whether you like it or not, a courageous person would get help before the one who is timid and weak.

Activity Four – You Can't Be 100% Ready

There are some setbacks you don't see coming, and they can be very devastating when they hit you. That's one thing you have to understand as you journey through life so that you don't wear yourself out with standards that are impossible to attain.

Activity Five – It's Okay To Stay Down For A While

It would be a different situation entirely if you saw it coming. But if you didn't, you may have to chill for a bit. Not forever, though. Just a little break enough to get you back in some shape.

Activity Six – Confide In People

It could be a partner, parent, or friend. It's possible to draw strength from them while maintaining yours. Never be too shy to talk if you can't take it all in. You don't want to go crazy, do you?

Activity Seven – Celebrate Your Wins

Yes! I repeat this. When you're finally able to get through that situation, give yourself some credit. It boosts your morale and assures you that you can do it through the next challenge.

Week Sixteen – Adopting The Virtues Of Goodness And Compassion

Activity One – Understanding The Virtues Of Goodness and Compassion

Having goodness and compassion means being generous and kind to people around you. With your words and with your actions without expecting anything in return.

Activity Two – Understand Why You Should Be Good To People

Doing an act of kindness from a genuine heart makes you happy and fulfilled. That's enough reason to be good to people. Imagine what joy you'd feel when you see the smile on the face of an older woman who you just gave alms. That alone can make your day!

Activity Three – Saying Kind Words

The tongue can cut like a knife if misused. You don't know what that person might be going through. Always be kind with your words. You might be saving a life.

Activity Four – Kind Deeds

You can take out a day or two in the week to carry out acts of kindness. It could be to those you know or not. It doesn't have to cost much—the thought counts.

Activity Five – Acts Of Services

In your workplace, around where you live, in your school, anywhere you find yourself, don't be hesitant to act out acts of service. It could be cleaning the neighborhood or running errands for a coworker.

Activity Six – Be Kind With Your Time

Though it may look immaterial, time is an essential aspect of human life, and being kind with your time will mean a lot to those who'd value it.

Activity Seven – Be Kind To Yourself

While you're being kind to other people, you've got to be kind to yourself. Take yourself out on treats, constantly remind yourself how special you are, and don't let anyone look down on you.

Week Seventeen – Adopting the Virtue of Practical Wisdom

Activity One – Understanding The Virtue of Practical Wisdom

Practical wisdom means knowing how to balance conflicting principles. This kind of wisdom acknowledges that uncertain risk cannot be avoided but guides us in becoming wiser about how we manage it.

Activity Two – Understanding The Need For Practical Wisdom

This virtue helps you balance your risk and take decisions that wouldn't cost much if anything goes south. It is a handy tool when you're at crossroads.

Activity Three – Acknowledge The Need For Practical Wisdom

The need for something creates a longing to get it by all means possible. Everyone needs to know what practical wisdom is, and you'd not be doing yourself a favor by lying to yourself that you don't need it.

Activity Four – Read Books

Books are a very reliable source of knowledge, but you have to make sure you're reading the right ones. Dedicate a month to complete a book, jot down what you've learned, and visit them regularly.

Activity Five – Seek Advice From Experienced People

There's no harm in going to others to seek advice. It's better than going headlong into what you know nothing about and failing.

Activity Six – Learn From Experience

Your past is a teacher. Please take advantage of everything it has to teach you because you paid heavily for it with the consequences of any mistake you made back then.

Activity Seven: Put What You've Learnt Into Practice.

Don't just sit there learning. Why would it be called Practical Wisdom when you're not going to act? The real benefit of your knowledge is in its application. Never forget that.

Week Eighteen – Adopting The Virtue of Humility

Activity One – Understanding The Virtue Of Humility

Humility is the virtue of being humble and putting another person's interest over yours. But don't be quick to equate this to having low self-esteem. That's far from it.

Activity Two – Understanding The Need To Be Humble

Humility is an attractive virtue, and it creates a very enabling environment for people around you. No one wants to be around a cocky person who would make people feel less of themselves. I will be highlighting a few ways to practice humility across the remaining activities.

Activity Three – Listening To Others.

Others would see what you may be doing wrong before you do. Always give listening ears to what others have to say to you. It allows you to learn more about yourself.

Activity Four – Cultivate The Act Of Gratitude

Be grateful for what you have and what you've achieved. I get it. You may have had a lot to do with your success, but don't ever forget that some force beyond the physical has enabled you to achieve that which others failed at.

Activity Five – Ask For Help When You Need It

Don't die in silence. If you need help, reach out to others to help you through that difficult phase. You're not alone in this world, and in one way or the other, the impact of others must be felt in your life.

Activity Six – Don't Be Too Quick To Judge.

This activity applies to both other people and yourself. Why judge? You may have no idea what the person you're judging is going through. Be humble enough to accept the person while helping the person improve.

Activity Seven: Appreciate The Effort Of Others.

No matter how insignificant it may seem, You must appreciate the efforts of others because you may not be aware of what it took for that person to make such an effort.

Week Nineteen – Adopting The Virtue Of Honesty

Activity One – Understanding The Virtue Of Honesty

Honesty is the virtue of being truthful. To both yourself and others. Saying a thing as it is and not painting it to be something else.

Activity Two – Understanding The Need For Honesty.

You must understand that being honest makes you a more reliable and trustworthy person. It also creates a safe space around you for others to seek opinions.

Activity Three – Staying True To Yourself

Stop trying to be something you're not. It rubs you off your originality, and the world loses your peculiarity because you've become another person.

Activity Four: You Don't Need To Be Brutally Honest.

When telling someone the truth, how you say it to the person is as crucial as the truth itself. You have to say to them as lovingly as possible. Make sure the person doesn't get hurt in the process.

Activity Five – Being Transparent In Your Dealings

Nobody likes a cunning person. If you're not honest in your way of life, no one would want anything to do with you and will be hesitant to offer help when you need it.

Activity Six – Company of Like Minds.

While you strive to be honest, surround yourself with real people. In such a formative period of your life, any form of negativity would dissuade you.

Activity Seven – Embrace Being Honest

Some people are scared of being honest because of what others may have to say. But that shouldn't bother you. You're fighting for the purity of your conscience, and what other people say should matter as long as you're doing the right thing.

Week Twenty – Adopting The Virtue Of Love

Activity One – Understanding The Virtue Of Love

Love is a deep feeling of affection towards a person or yourself. It encompasses some of what we've discussed previously, so this is probably like a recap of the discussion so far.

Activity Two – Forgiveness

You must be willing to forgive those you love and accept yourself more. You have to forgive yourself as well.

Activity Three – Honesty

When you love a person, you seek the overall improvement of such a person, and being honest will help you achieve that.

Activity Four – Goodness/Compassion

When you are in a position to help, it becomes straightforward to help such a person out in times of their need or even randomly.

Activity Five – Patience

Loving a person requires a lot of patience, tolerance, and overlooking a lot of things that are supposed to get you riled up.

Activity Six – Commitment

Commitment is the virtue of being dedicated to a particular cause. Loving a person requires you to be committed to that person's growth and welfare.

Activity Seven – Respect

In this context, we'd be referring to having regard for the feeling of others. You must understand that not everyone would be comfortable with everything you love doing. Recognizing this and acting goes a long way in telling how much you love a person.

Week Twenty-One: Spirituality and Humanitarianism

This week is about learning intensively, so in addition to all I'll be saying throughout the week, I urge you to do extensive research on the following concepts I will briefly talk about.

One week will be majorly theory, while the subsequent week will be practical. I've made it that way so that you find your weeks completely fun, educational, and practicable.

Activity One – Understanding The Concept of Humanitarianism

Although the word isn't so common in everyday usage, I believe you must have heard of it. Today's activity is that you research the meaning of Humanitarianism. I'll give a brief definition, and you can check out others. Wikipedia defines Humanitarianism to be an active belief in the value of human life and the practice of humane treatment and provision of assistance to humans to reduce their suffering. Now, you can pick it up from there.

Activity Two – Relating Humanitarianism To Spirituality

Spirituality is about your connection to your true self, and it extends outwardly and helps you connect with others on a whole new level. When you've attained spirituality, the virtue of benevolence to humans wouldn't be so hard. Find time to get a note on how being a humanitarian can boost your spirituality and vice versa.

Activity Three - Concept Of Tribalism

Ordinarily, the concept of tribalism meant the advocacy for tribes and their lifestyles. But it's now associated with the negative part, which defines it as hostilities towards particular tribes by other groups. Research more on tribalism and instances where it has caused grave damage to people.

Activity Four – Humanitarianism Fights Against Tribalism

Based on the above concept of tribalism to be either advocacy for tribes or hostilities against tribes, Humanitarianism seeks to bring peace amongst various warring tribes and encourage harmony between all tribes. Learn about how Humanitarianism has affected the negative aspects of tribalism in today's world.

Activity Five – Concept Of Slavery

We'll learn about the history of slavery, and I'm keen on seeing you make the best out of this topic. I'll set aside an entire week for activities in which you'll learn about the history and power of black people. But for today's action, I only desire you to learn about the general history of slavery in the world.

Activity Six – Humanitarianism Fights Against Slavery

Slavery might sound archaic because that's how it seems, but did you ever think about the narrative that, although repressed, it still exists and is even revolutionized? That's by the way, though. Before we conclude the week's activities tomorrow, write out ten humanitarians who fought against slavery and try to learn about them.

Activity Seven – Humanitarianism Fights Against Discrimination

Oh, how much I love this part because it would lead us to the practical aspect of this topic for week twenty-one. For today, learn extensively about discrimination, ways people discriminate, and how we can reduce discrimination in our society.

Week Twenty-Two: Practicing Humanitarianism

Activity One – Reach Out

You don't have to fret about the tasks for this week as they'll be straightforward.

Please take notice of a person or persons who always seem left out in your place of work or school and talk to them. Just interact.

Activity Two – Visitations

Find time in your schedule to visit someone in the hospital who is probably, sick, recovering, or nursing. You can also opt to see an older adult who's usually alone.

Activity Three – Invitations

If you're not comfortable with visiting people or do not have the time but prefer accepting visits in your home, you could host a meal and invite a homeless person or less privileged to eat with you.

Activity Four – Donations

You could donate domestic equipment, your blood, toiletry supplies, toys, food boxes, etc. Also, go for other ideas about local donations that come to your mind.

Activity Five – Writing

Publishing articles on Humanitarianism that help enlighten people about the concept and promote it amongst them is a great way. Writing and simply sharing on social media is also a great idea.

Activity Six – Babysitting

Offering to babysit a child whose parents are extremely busy is also a way of showing Love to humans. You can also watch over teenagers and give them good advice.

Activity Seven – Campaign

You can hold a campaign to promote Humanitarianism and broaden people's knowledge on why we should show compassion to ourselves and aim to be better persons.

Week Twenty-Three: Signs To Look For In Spiritual Persons

You might need to talk to certain persons or make friends with people who would help and encourage you on your spiritual journey. The following are ways to recognize a spiritual person.

Activity One – Recognition Of Self

If there's anyone you have in mind to be your mentor or spiritual friend, you have to be able to know if they recognize themselves in others. Do they see themselves as one with all beings, things, and creatures and therefore trail the path of Love and compassion towards all beings? If you see yourself as one with someone, would you want to hurt yourself?

Activity Two – Sincerity And Humility

I want to share this quote by Nisargadatta with you. I found it captivating, so here; "When I look within and see that I am nothing, that's wisdom. When I look out and see that I am everything, that's Love. Between these two, my life turns."

Spiritual people know who they are in this world and understand the need to remain humble and sincere to themselves.

Activity Three – True Lovers

Observe a spiritual person and notice how they love. There are no strings attached, and they love freely. They're the embodiment of Love and radiate it in its glory. A spiritual person would not wait for you to show Love to them before they reciprocate. Neither would they stop if you don't return. They are children of Love.

Activity Four – Trust

Spiritual Persons do not worry unnecessarily about what tomorrow holds but rather believe and hope that things will fall in place. They allow life to lead the way.

Activity Five – Search For Their Forgiving Spirit

Spiritual Persons do not expect humans to be perfect and therefore are more than willing to forgive them when they err or mistreat them. This virtue is rare as most people harbor hate in them, so you'll be lucky to find someone with a forgiving spirit.

Activity Six – Generous Hearts

At some point, you may need a favor from your spiritual friend, and one of the ways you can know that they're in tune with their spirituality is in their generosity of heart, giving without asking back.

Activity Seven – Quietness And Solitude

All spiritual persons love to meditate, so this should be easy to spot. I can imagine how happy you would be when you find someone who loves quietness just as you do!

Week Twenty-Four: Spirituality and Environmentalism

Activity One – Understanding The Concept Of Environmentalism

This week is going to be just like week twenty. I hope you remember how it went and all you practiced concerning Humanitarianism. Environmentalism is the concern and actions expressed by people to protect the environment. We'll be doing a lot of theory and practice this week. So today, research on the meaning and history of environmentalism.

Activity Two – Relating Environmentalism To Spirituality

Today will be about understanding the link spirituality has with environmentalism. The knowledge that spirituality has to do with finding our true selves and being in tune with nature is enough for you to begin linking these two concepts together.

Activity Three – Reflection On Our Actions

I'll ask three questions, and you let me fill your journal with seven more reflection questions.

"How do you view the environment around you?"

"Have you supported environmental pollution by your actions, inactions, or words?"

"How do you dispose of your dirt?"

Activity Four – Global Warming

You can write out the definition of global warming, the causes, and the effects. I'll give three examples of global warming:

Shifts in the blooming of flowers.

Continuous decrease in the extent of ice and snow.

Dirtier air.

Activity Five – Steps To Environmentalism

With the assumption that you've studied environmentalism, global warming, and other pollution, the next three days from today will be on the commitment to keeping your environment clean.

For today, conserve water.

Activity Six – Practice The 3Rs

The 3Rs, which I'd like to call Reduce, Reuse, and Recycle, are ways to make your environment better. Reduce the inessential things you buy. Make sure to reuse items that can be reused rather than throwing them away, and lastly, Recycle.

Activity Seven – Conserve Electricity

Research on ways to conserve electricity. Start today with switching off the lights when not in use.

Week Twenty-Five: Practicing Environmental Care

Activity One – Plant a tree today.

Activity Two – Conserve Water

Fix a leaking pipe.

Collect water from the rain and water your lawn with it another day.

Don't leave the tap running while brushing your teeth.

Activity Three – Go environmentally friendly with a Rooftop Solar Photovoltaic (PV). It's affordable.

Activity Four – Change all your bulbs to LED light bulbs today. They last longer and use less power.

Activity Five – Stop wasting food intentionally and unintentionally. Try as much as possible to cook or buy what you can finish.

Activity Six – Use fewer products made of fossil fuels.

Activity Seven – Take a stroll to the nearest grocery store nearby and buy locally grown products. They're completely healthy, plus you're supporting local farms and dairies.

Week Twenty-Six: Spirituality and Mental Health

Activity One – Understanding You're More Important

The most important person in your life is you—work towards truly understanding this and see how much you'd love yourself.

Activity Two – Speak Up

If you're still bothered about something after twenty-four hours, speak up within forty-eight hours.

Activity Three – Stop The Addiction

You could be excessively doing consciously or unconsciously in an attempt to numb pain. But don't you think it's better to speak out or talk to someone about how you truly feel than to do things that would harm you?

Activity Four: Don't Apologize For What You Feel.

Often, you might feel a specific way about something or someone and end up apologizing because you expressed it. If you say it entirely civilized, you do not have to apologize.

It's okay to be sad, happy, terrified, anxious, or any other emotion. You shouldn't apologize for how you feel. Try to build your self-esteem with this and exercise self-control towards your feelings.

Activity Five – You Are Responsible For Yourself

Forget that you have a husband, wife, children, or friend. Do you care for yourself as much as you do for them? Do you take out time for yourself? Giving yourself time gives you peace and helps you connect more with your family and friends.

Activity Six – Go Through Your Pain

Rather than walking away or trying to numb your pain, you should go through it. That way, you're able to overcome it and become stronger.

Activity Seven – Seek Help

When you look at it, asking for help is one of the best steps to success. Rather than doing it all on your own, why not talk to someone to help you with it, help you overcome that feeling? To your greatest surprise, some people want to help.

Week Twenty-Seven: Fixing Your Mental Health

Activity One – Write out ten Affirmations on self-love.

Activity Two – Talk to someone about what they did to offend or hurt you.

Activity Three – Go a day without something you're addicted to. Celebrate that feat and try reducing the addiction.

Activity Four – Meditate today. Write out ten valuable things about yourself.

Activity Five – Do something that involves going through your pain and not walking away from it.

Activity Six – Treat yourself to a nice meal.

Activity Seven – Talk to a friend, family member, or a professional about your feelings.

Week Twenty-Eight: Practicing Self-awareness

Activity One: Meditate on your thoughts daily.

Activity Two: Listen to what others have to say about you.

Activity Three: Travel to places and watch your reactions to these places.

Activity Four: Learn a new skill that would enable you to think and act originally.

Activity Five: Observe what you blurt out when stressed or angry and become more aware of yourself.

Activity Six: Do a quick reflection and write five values you hold in high esteem.

Activity Seven: Try writing fiction or reading a fictional story and observe how you think about certain things.

Week Twenty-Nine: Defining Your Happiness

Activity One – Loving Yourself

When you love and cherish yourself, which spirituality teaches you to, it would be hard to be shaken by what others say or do to you?

Activity Two – Helping Others

Carry out a kind action today.

Activity Three – Acceptance

Look at yourself in the mirror and notice how beautiful you are. Learn to accept all your flaws.

Activity Four – Transcending Materialism

Ask yourself questions about how materialistic you are.

Determine today not to place your happiness on material things.

Activity Five – Celebrate

Write out ten things you achieved the previous week and think of a way to celebrate your success.

Activity Six – Do What You Love

List five things you love doing every time. Make sure to do them every day if possible and keep track of this.

Activity Seven – Make Good Friends

If your friends aren't making you happy, it's time to surround yourself with better people.

Week Thirty: Generosity week!

Activity One – Gifts

Buy someone a dress.

Write someone a handwritten note.

Pay for a stranger's coffee.

Please include some more, my beautiful black woman.

Activity Two – Learning Kind Words

"You always excel at what you do!"

"You are so brave!"

"You are a beautiful human, and I don't mean only on the external. You have a big heart."

Activity Three – Visit A Retirement Home

Go with gifts, of course, and interact with the elderly. Listen to them talk about their experiences, and be sure to get a few life tips from them. You can even ask someone to guide you on your path to spirituality.

Activity Four – Alternatives To Money

If you want to give someone something as an act of kindness this week but do not have the money for it.

Here are three alternatives, and of course, you could add yours.

Donate blood to a hospital.

Volunteer your time to the development of your community.

Donate extra belongings. It could be clothes, toys, or pieces of equipment you no longer need.

Activity Five – Compliments

Today is for compliments. Get your journal out and decide to compliment ten strangers today. Please fill up your diary with your choice of compliments and the replies from each of them. This activity should be fun.

Activity Six – Determine To Be Patient

Here's another practice for you. Write out the number of times you got angry over something this week. You don't have to stress over remembering everything. Just the few you remember are okay. Now take up the challenge not to flare up over a trivial issue. Best of luck, brave woman!

Activity Seven: Have some rest.

You've done so much this week, giving, and giving, and I'm proud of you for your progress. You deserve all the rest you can get, but don't forget that each activity is a continuous process. You're not to stop just because the week runs out and another begins with new activities.

Overall, have some fun today and laugh more.

Week Thirty-One: Voicing Out Affirmations 2

It's another special week where we'll be voicing out affirmations. I'll list out three affirmations as usual, and you can add as much as you wish.

Activity One – Affirmations For Leaders

"I am a role model to people, an inspiration."

"I know I can and will make a positive change."

"People will remember me for good."

Activity Two – Affirmations For Black Women

"I love how dark my skin is."

"I know how unique my hair texture is. That's why I'm in love with it."

"I will enact the change I desire."

Activity Three – Affirmations For Working Moms

"My children love and see me as a great parent."

"I make a difference in my family."

"I am supportive and a powerhouse."

Activity Four – Affirmations For Confidence

"I can do difficult tasks."

"I am bright and articulate."

"I believe I can do this."

Activity Five – Affirmations For Honoring Your Achievements

"I am proud of all I've achieved."

"My friends and family will be so proud of me."

"I am a winner, a conqueror."

Activity Six – Affirmations For a Healthy Mindset

"I believe in my abilities."

"I feel safe, happy, and content."

"I am in control of my reaction to others."

Activity Seven – Affirmations For Relationships

"I love my partner."

"I do not envy my partner's success but wish to see them grow."

"I do not have doubts about my partner's fidelity."

Week Thirty-Two: Growing Your Business

Activity One – Meditation

Meditation is a required method of growing your business. Dedicating time to yourself for meditation helps you become aware of yourself and your purpose.

Meditation opens your mind to new ideas for your business.

Activity Two – Humility

Nobody likes a person who is proud and boastful. Understand that you're just one in the world and need people to fulfill your existence. So when things are going great for you, don't let it get into your head.

Activity Three – Be Gracious

In all you do, radiate light wherever you are. As you carry out your duties in your business place, do them graciously. Strive to stand out amongst your peers and competitors.

Activity Four – Say Sorry When You Should

If you wrong your customers or fellow humans, apologize instantly and suppress the urge to make up excuses.

Activity Five – Practice Forgiveness

When someone offends you, it's ideal that you let them know and forgive them instantly, whether they apologize. Forgiving people help your mind to stay healthy and encourages your growth.

Activity Six – Stop Limiting Your Thoughts

Deliberately or subconsciously limiting your thoughts and letting doubts is a road to failure. Allow your mind to express its creativity.

Activity Seven – Be Positive

Treat people kindly always, no matter how they may be. When you treat all kinds of people nicely, it makes them feel like you believe in them, possibly that they can be good.

Week Thirty-Three: Spirituality and Career Development

Activity One – Express Positivity

When your co-workers are feeling down due to things happening in your workplace, it's your duty as a spiritual person to offer them comfort and hope that things will get better.

Activity Two – Take Some Time Out

If you're feeling too tired from working continuously, it's okay to take a break. Remember always to meditate.

Activity Three – Connect With Your Co-workers

Being a spiritual person is about connecting with your true self and others, and a great place to connect with people is at your workplace. Bake pie and share with your co-workers, ask them how their day is going, etc.

Activity Four – Share Ideas With Your Boss

It wouldn't be nice if you have a great idea but choose to keep it to yourself. Think of ideas that would boost the company's values and success.

Activity Five – Use Words Carefully

When angry, take a breath before speaking. When stressed, breathe in and out. With any negative emotion you feel within you, always take a breath to think of what to say. Words can scar people for life, so you might want to choose your words more carefully.

Activity Six – Reflection

Take time to reflect on your progress since you started working for the company. Think of things you could do to be rewarded with a promotion. Also, congratulate yourself on your progress so far.

Activity Seven – Host A Party

In the spirit of connecting with your co-workers, hosting a party is a great idea to get together and relax after work.

Week Thirty-Four: Living Healthy Lifestyles

Activity One – Drink More Water

Activity Two – Eat Fruits And Vegetables

Whenever you're at the grocery store, always get fruits to eat after your meal.

Activity Three – Avoid Harboring Negativity

Stop doubting your potential. Stop harboring hate and all other negative emotions. Let go of the negativity in your life.

Activity Four – Get Enough Sleep

If you've not been getting enough sleep, you're not living healthily. Sleep for at least eight hours today and every other day.

Activity Five – Walk Away From Negative People

Avoid people who, rather than encourage you to achieve your goals, laugh at them and invalidate your feelings. Avoid people who cause you pain intentionally and unintentionally.

Activity Six - Stop smoking or consuming hard drugs.

Activity Seven - Go to a park with friends and family.

Week Thirty-Five: Encouraging Words For Sick People

Visit a sick person this week and offer encouraging words to them.

Some encouraging words are:

"I hope you get better soon."

"It's a healing process. Don't rush things."

"Looking forward to seeing you back at work when you're better."

"You're in my thoughts every day as you recover from your illness."

"I love you and think of you all the time."

"I realize just how much I need you. So be strong for me!"

"You've been so brave handling this. You're my hero."

Week Thirty-Six: Dealing With Negative Feelings: Jealousy

Activity One – Find The Source

Think about your jealousy and the reason for it. You ought to have an idea of what the source is. When you do, please write it down.

Activity Two – Talk About Your Feelings

If your partner is doing something to make you feel jealous, you should talk about it with them, or you could talk about the source of your jealousy with someone you trust.

Activity Three – Turn The Negative Into Positive

Rather than let jealousy get the best of you. Decide to do positive things with it. If you're jealous of your best friend's new car, turn that jealousy into a passion and work towards getting a car for yourself too.

Activity Four – Look At Things From Another Perspective

What if there's no justification for you to be jealous. You're probably jealous of someone's fortune, but did you stop to wonder if they're unhappy with it?

Activity Five – Gratitude

Today, I need you to flashback to all you learned about gratitude during week seven's activities. Practice them today.

Activity Six – Take A Break

If you're working on overcoming something that triggers your jealousy, I suggest you take a break from it and things related to it. Also, walk away if you can.

Activity Seven – Always Take A Deep Breath

Feeling overwhelmed with thoughts of jealousy, take a deep breath and release. Repeat this process to calm your mind.

Week Thirty-Seven: Dealing With Negative Feelings: Anger

Activity One – Take Your Time To Think

When you're upset, you can say terrible things that people may never forget, so take your time to think thoroughly before speaking when provoked.

Activity Two – Express Your Anger Calmly

Try to calm yourself before expressing yourself. You could take a few breaths in, count from one to ten, walk away from the trigger. Just call yourself.

Activity Three – Exercise

If you're on the verge of getting angry, it's okay to take a walk or run.

Activity Four – Declare Positive Affirmations

"I can feel myself getting angry, but I choose to stay in control."

"I will remember to pause, stop and think before carrying out any action."

"I will not allow myself to perform an action I will regret."

Activity Five – Express Humor

Try listening to a joke when you're angry or even force yourself to laugh.

Activity Six – Let Go Of Grudges

Rather than piling up so much grudge in your heart, talk to the people who offended you about what they did.

Activity Seven – Seek Help

If you have an extreme anger issue, it's best to seek professional help.

Week Thirty-Eight: Dealing With Negative Feelings: Guilt

Activity One – Name Your Guilt

For example, *"I cheated on someone, and I feel terrible about it."*

"I feel bad that I yelled at a stranger who didn't deserve it."

Activity Two – Write Out The Roots Of It

Guilt could stem from things you've done, haven't done, or guilt-tripping from someone.

Activity Three – Apologize

Yes, say one of the magic words and tell the person you're sorry without making excuses.

Activity Four – Make Amends

It could be that your apology isn't enough at times, so go the extra mile to show that you're genuinely sorry. Make amends.

Activity Five – Learn

It could also be that whatever you did or whatever happened cannot be amended, so all you can choose to do is to learn from the past.

Activity Six – Gratitude

Oh yes, we're here again. Tell people you're thankful.

Activity Seven – Forgive Yourself

One of the things prolonging that guilt you always feel is guilt. Please, my dear black woman, forgive yourself.

Week Thirty-Nine: Dealing With Negative Feelings: Fear

Activity One - Take a deep breath in.

Activity Two – Learn about your fear

It might turn out that what you're afraid of really isn't anything to fear.

Activity Three – Stop Imagining Negative Things

Rather than expanding your fear by imagining the negative, use your imagination positively. Imagine happy places.

Activity Four - Engage in frequent meditations.

Activity Five – Be In Nature More Often

When you can't get the chance to talk to a therapist or friend about your fear, you could have some alone time in nature.

Activity Six - Use Your Fear To Your Advantage

Activity Seven – Make Goals

Write out five goals to achieve concerning your fear. For example, "I will address the crowd that I've feared all my life."

Week Forty: Dealing With Negative Feelings: Depression

Activity One – Don't Wallow Too Long

One of the reasons people fall into depression is wallowing too much in their sorrow. Feel that sadness but don't let it engulf you.

Activity Two – Embrace Hope

If what's currently happening is the cause of your depression, accept that tomorrow is unknown and be hopeful about it.

Activity Three – Stop Overgeneralizing

Stop thinking about all the wrong things in your life every time you forget that there have been some good times.

Activity Four – Drop That Weapon

There might be a voice that urges you to self-inflict. Do the exact opposite, drop that weapon.

Activity Five – Take A Break

Take a break from things stressing you out and adding to your depression.

Activity Six – Distract Yourself

Whenever you have depressive thoughts, take a walk, listen to music or chit-chat with a friend. Do things to distract you.

Activity Seven - Find a hobby you love doing.

Week Forty-One: Starting A Friendship

Activity One – Join A Group

Find a group with similar interests as yours and meet with them regularly.

Activity Two – Talk To Them

If you're interested in being friends with someone, you can start talking to them.

Activity Three – Accept Invitations

If you're invited by someone to hang out with them or a group of friends, it's okay to accept as long as you feel comfortable around them.

Activity Four – Smile Often

Activity Five – Talk About Yourself

If you're going to be friends with someone, they will have to know you, so you will feel okay talking about yourself with them. Also, ask them about themselves.

Activity Six – Carry Out Favors

The favors may seem little to you. It could be preparing their favorite meal, calling to ask how they are, etc. Show that you care.

Activity Seven – Don't Fake It.

It would be best if you didn't fake who you aren't to be friends with someone.

Week Forty-Two: Sustaining Friendships

Activity One - Call a friend you haven't heard from in a while.

Activity Two - Get a gift for each of your family members.

Activity Three - Get a gift for your friend.

Activity Four - Think of three friends that mean the world to you and write out five things you like about them.

Activity Five - Be honest with your friends.

If there's anyone you've lied to in the past, let them in on today's truth.

Activity Six – Encourage them.

If any of your friends are going through a lot now, send an encouraging message and let them know you care.

Activity Seven – Visitations

Most friendships grow stronger through communication and meetings. Call your friends and also try to visit the ones you can. You can also invite them to spend time with you.

Week Forty-Three: Getting Into A Relationship

Activity One – Be Clear About Your Intentions

Don't just get into relationships with people because of what you feel. Be certain of what you want with them and let them know. Know what they want too.

Activity Two – Have Self-Respect

Have respect for yourself and love yourself first. That way, you can respect and love someone else and know when someone is being unserious with you.

Activity Three – Move On

Write out things you need to move on from and work towards them before entering a relationship.

Activity Four – Avoid Peer Pressure

Don't enter a relationship because you're being pressured to. Be certain it's what you want.

Activity Five – Accept Your Partner

You shouldn't go into a relationship hoping that your partner will change a certain behavior. Either you accept their flaws and all or let them be.

Activity Six – Communicate

When you think about them, place a call and let them know they crossed your mind. Keep it moderate, though.

Activity Seven – Hang Out

Go to places with them and, observe how they react to things, note what they like and don't like. See if you feel at peace with them or not.

Week Forty-Four: Sustaining Your Relationship

Activity One – Continue The Communication

Don't relax because you're now dating or married to your partner. Still talk to them as much as you used to. Also, talk about things that matter to you both.

Activity Two – Be Dependable

Be someone your partner would always want to run to when they're troubled. Be someone they feel safe with.

Activity Three – Treat Yourself

Take out today to treat yourself specially. You can even ask your partner to take you on a treat.

Activity Four – Give Your Partner A Treat

Today is for your partner. Take them on a special treat and watch them smile throughout the day.

Activity Five – Say The Magic Words

"I'm sorry."

"Please."

"Thank you."

"You're welcome."

Activity Six – Spend Time With Your Partner

Create time out of your busy schedule to be with them. You could stay at home and watch a movie or play games or even go to a restaurant or their favorite place with them.

Activity Seven – Don't Be So Uptight.

Nobody wants to be around people who are always uptight and never find humor in anything. Do funny things, laugh with your partner and be happy.

Week Forty-Five: Understanding Sex and Sexual Intercourse

Activity One – Learn The Meaning

Write out the meaning of sex in your journal. Here's one meaning of sex from the Oxford Dictionary: a "sexual activity, including specifically sexual intercourse." You can research other definitions.

Activity Two – Know The types Of Sex

There are different kinds of sex. Vaginal, oral, anal sex, etc. Know about them.

Activity Three – Libido

What is libido?

How is it affected?

What affects it?

Activity Four – Learn About Consent

Consent is a very important keyword associated with sex. Learn about what it is and why it's important.

Activity Five – Use A Condom

Know about the type of protection to use when having sex to avoid STIs.

Activity Six – Learn About STIs

Know the full meaning of STIs. What they are, how they're transmitted, the stigma that follows, and everything about the topic.

Activity Seven – Know Your Partner's Sexual Choices

Learn about how your partner would rather have sex, which they would have sex with, do they have a fetish, etc.

Week Forty-Six: Preparing For Sex

Activity One – Give Hints

Let your partner know that you'd want to have sex before having sex, to avoid being unprepared.

Activity Two – Use Condoms

To avoid the transmission of STIs, always have a condom with you.

Activity Three – Lubricant Is Essential

Keep a lubricant next to your bed for easy reach while having sex.

Activity Four – Relax

You shouldn't have sex if you don't feel like it or feel tensed up. Try to relax first.

Activity Five – Slow And Steady

Starting slow will place you completely in the mood for sex and allow for easy penetration. Let your partner know that there's no need to rush.

Activity Six – Communicate Your Needs

If there's something you need before or while having sex, let your partner know. Always communicate if you need them to go faster or slower or stop completely.

Activity Seven – Spend Time With Your Partner

You do not necessarily have to talk always. Just snuggling up next to your partner and cuddling is needed sometimes.

Week Forty-Seven: Spicing Up Your Sex Life With Your Partner

Activity One – Keep your clothes on

Try something new. Rather than taking off your clothes completely, you could take off a few pieces and leave some. It can make you appear sexier to your partner.

Activity Two – Use Lubricant!

Using a flavored lubricant would make your partner want to go down completely on you for a very long time. It's great for sex.

Activity Three – Switch Locations.

Don't be boring. Try out different places for sex.

Activity Four - Try new positions with your partner.

It could be a wheelbarrow, 69, The leapfrog, etc.

Activity Five – Masturbate

Understand your body and know what makes you orgasm. That way, you can guide your partner.

Activity Six - Using a vibrator isn't a bad idea. Buy a premium one for better sex.

Activity Seven – Write Out Your Fantasies

Try to be creative and think about ways you'd like to have sex. Show your partner and agree on what to do together. Overall, have fun.

Week Forty-Eight: Voicing Out Affirmations 3

Activity One – Affirmations For Sexual Confidence

"I embrace my sexuality and accept who I am."

"I am breathtaking."

"I deserve the gift of sexual pleasure."

Activity Two – Affirmations For Body Positivity

"I won't starve myself in a bid to get a slimmer body."

"I love every part of my body and think they're awesome."

"Comparing myself to others is a sign of low-self esteem. I won't cultivate that habit."

Activity Three – Affirmations For Beauty

"I love my eyes. They're captivating."

"I am incredibly sexy."

"I love my black skin because it's beautiful."

Activity Four – Affirmations For A Great Sex Life

"My body makes my partner go wild whenever he sees me."

"My body deserves all the touches, caresses and pleasure it gets."

"Sex is a sacred activity that the partner I choose and I have decided to engage in."

Activity Five – Affirmations For Sex Drive

"I am charged with sexual energy."

"I accept sex as a part of my life."

"None of my sexual experiences will be bland."

Activity Six – Affirmations For Seduction

"I am tuned in to male/female signals."

"I am confident with my partner."

"My seduction skills are becoming powerful."

Activity Seven – Affirmations For Dating

"I am worthy of love and respect that anyone gives."

"I will find the perfect one who would love and cherish me."

"I am capable of giving love to people."

Week Forty-Nine: Embracing Your Sexuality

Activity One – Do What Makes You Happy

Rather than worry about what people would say about your sexuality, why not do what makes you happy, what you care about? Dance in a weird way, dress crazily, whatever makes you happy.

Activity Two – Embrace Your Body

If you're putting on clothes to avoid seeing your body, then you have to stop. Observe and admire yourself in the mirror and smile at how beautiful you are.

Activity Three – Fall In Love With Yourself

For you to love someone, you have to love yourself first. Remember your spiritual journey.

Activity Four – Stop Following The Media

The media says to do this, and you do it even to your unhappiness. That's a really bad path to follow. Stop listening to people who have barely lived their life telling you how to live yours.

Activity Five – Sex Positivity

Listen to podcasts like Why Are People Into That, read Lisa Taddeo's Three Women. Follow books that encourage sex-positivity.

Activity Six – You Should Feel Great

Sexuality and sex should make you feel great and not less of yourself. So if you feel otherwise after having sex with your partner, it's a sign that's not it.

Activity Seven – Accept Your Sexuality

Understand that God isn't ashamed of your sexuality because he made you who you are. So if he's okay with it, why shouldn't you be?

Week Fifty: Preparing For A Vacation

I planned a vacation for you for weeks fifty-one to fifty-two, which is two weeks. I don't know what time is suitable for you so that you can adjust it. But my dear black woman, try as much as you can to go on a vacation before the year runs out. Take a rest and feel refreshed.

Activity One – Save Up

Start by planning your budget and saving up for your vacation.

Activity Two – Ask Questions

Wherever you have in mind to travel to, it's best to do your research on it, foods you could try, places you could go, etc.

Activity Three – Use A Checklist

As you pack, you mustn't overpack and also not under-pack. So have a checklist which you would work with to ensure you pack all you need.

Activity Four – Check The Weather

Some countries might have unfavorable weather by the time you wish to travel. Do your best to check the weather and plan according to it.

Activity Five - Pay off any outstanding bills before you leave.

Rather than piling up your bills while away, it's best to pay them off. You're going on a vacation to refresh your body and mind; it wouldn't be nice to return refreshed only to be cramped up with bills to pay.

Activity Six – Notify Your Bank

It would help if you always remembered to call your bank and inform them of your travel days and where you're traveling to ensure your credit card remains active in the country you intend to visit.

Activity Seven – Leave Your Home In Shape

Unplug electronics, turn off the lights, turn off the tap, etc. Make sure your home is in order before traveling.

Week Fifty-One – Week Fifty-Two: Vacation Week!

Conclusion

My dear black woman, I had an exhilarating experience writing this book for you. I hope you had a fun time reading through it, too. I hope you learnt, and I hope all that you learned stays with you for a very long time.

Every day society tries to shun black women by telling them what their spirituality and sexuality should be and what they shouldn't be. But the truth remains that no one can define your spirituality for you. Same as your sexuality. These are two important things that you define and experience by yourself.

This book mirrors my journey as a black woman who chooses not to let the world affect her spiritual and sexual self. Every word is me telling my truth and living it. It took a long time to get this far.

I hope this book helps you too. I hope you become your most audacious, daring, spiritual, and adventurous self. You are so dearly and deeply loved.

www.ingramcontent.com/pod-product-compliance
Lightning Source LLC
Chambersburg PA
CBHW071730080526
44588CB00013B/1974